D1173925

'The poet with the painted wings'

Henry Miller

Walter Erben

Revised Edition

MARC CHAGALL

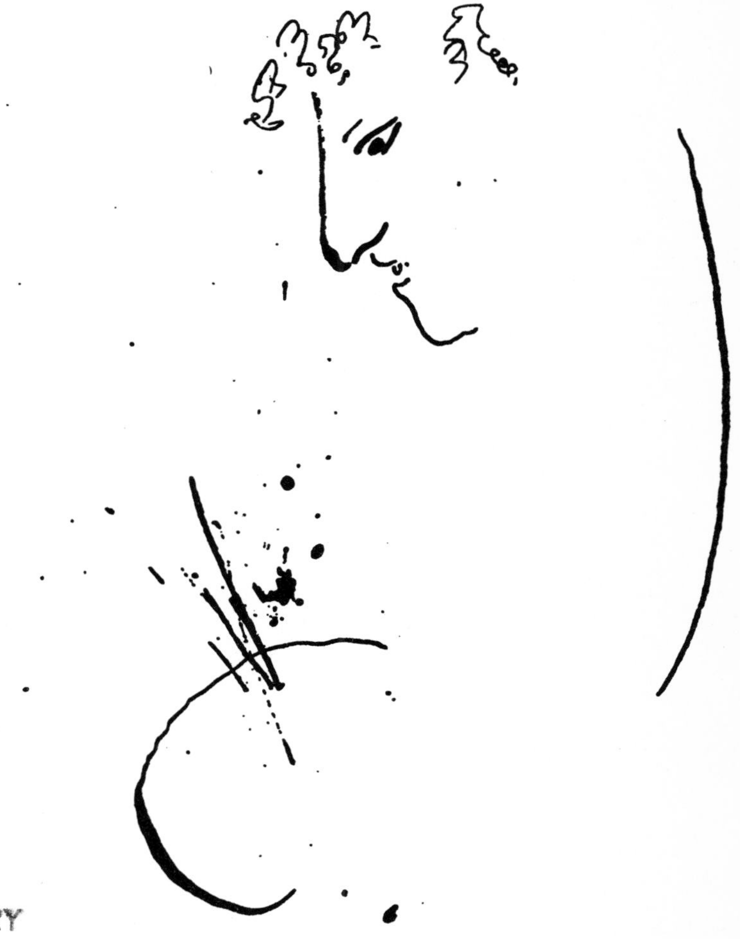

Frederick A. Praeger, Publishers

New York · Washington

Translated by Michael Bullock from the German edition
published by Prestel-Verlag, Munich

BOOKS THAT MATTER

Published in the United States of America in 1957
by Frederick A. Praeger, Inc., Publishers
111 Fourth Avenue, New York 3, N.Y.

Revised edition 1966

Library of Congress Catalog Card Number: 66 – 21776

Printed in Germany

CONTENTS

9 The Magician of Vence
20 In the Musée d'Art Moderne
22 'Churches, Fences, Shops, Synagogues...'
26 St Petersburg
29 Birth, Marriage, Death
32 Cubism
35 La Ruche
40 The Example of the Poets
42 Me and My Village
43 Plastic Sense
46 Paris through the Window
50 Calvary – Fervour for the Truth
54 Herwarth Walden and *Der Sturm*
56 Every Picture an Embrace
59 The Birthday
61 The Rabbi of Vitebsk
63 War and Revolution
70 The Jewish Theatre
76 Berlin 1922 – Etchings from *Mein Leben*
84 Return to Paris
85 An Honest Craftsman of God
88 The Discovery of Colour
92 The Fortunate Disaster
96 'Echoes of a Deeper Reality'
100 Rembrandt – Etchings for the *Bible*
104 Time is a River without Banks
109 Apocalypse of the Soul
111 Crucifixion-Martyrdom
115 Exile in the USA
119 'In the Shell of his Universe'
124 'Ringing Forms, Filled with Passion'
125 The Fire Bird
128 Pictures like Mighty Ikons
131 Thanks to Paris
134 'A Longing to Bind Oneself to this Earth'
138 The Harmonious Synthesis
140 'The Echo of an Art at once Close and Remote'
144 Visions of a Truer and More Beautiful World
148 '... des couleurs fraîches et brutes'
153 Epilogue – ten years later

To my wife and my children

The debt I owe to Mr. and Mrs. Chagall for the help they gave me in compiling this account has been expressed in the following pages. I feel equally indebted to Mrs. Ida Meyer-Chagall and Dr. Franz Meyer of Basle for the ready way in which they provided me with information. Earlier publications on Chagall were of great value to me during my work. I was permitted to make use of the painter's dicta and a wealth of biographical detail contained in the works of Efross-Tugendhold, James Johnson Sweeney, Raïssa Maritain and Dr. Isaac Kloomok. Mr. Sweeney's book, published by the Museum of Modern Art, New York, carries a detailed bibliography up to the year 1945. A biography taking the story up to 1961, together with a corresponding catalogue of Chagall's oeuvre, is contained in the definitive work on the artist by Dr. Franz Meyer, which has appeared in several languages. I am particularly anxious to draw attention to the completeness of authenticated facts offered by that work, since my own book, having quite a different object in view, does not attempt to be so thorough.

Walter Erben

Marc Chagall

You paint with a star instead of a brush
devour the head of the morning like ripe fruit
and bare the breasts of midnight
with a candle's ardour.
For you the meadow billows like a banner
cattle dance to a fiddle's laughter
tombstones lift their voices
in the exaltation of a cantor's chant.
Your nights of love blossom
into branches of lilac
till the cool of evening
becomes a blazing furnace.

Michael Bullock

The Magician of Vence

Madame Chagall had told me on the telephone that her husband would expect me at three o'clock. I arrived a few minutes earlier at the entrance to the park, at the far end of which the tall villa-like house and the front of the more modern studio sparkled among the greenery of tropical trees. One half of the wrought iron gate had swung open and was firmly wedged in the gravel. To the right, inside the head-high wall that ran round the property, a path lined with young cypresses led to the higher section of the park. The gravel of the drive dazzled the eyes. The trees stood in their own circular shadows; not a breath of air stirred their foliage. On the other side of the path, terraces rose one above the other and apple trees towered above the tangled grass. Their leaves were parched, but the fruit was round and ripe.

In the ivy of the gate-post hung a sign with carefully painted letters, 'Les Collines'. I did not want to wait inside the park, so I walked a little way up the road and sat down on a step in the gap of a neighbouring wall. The fleshy-fingered leafage of a walnut-tree cast its shadow above my head. A few hundred yards further along, beyond the *pensions* for foreign visitors, stood the Chapelle du Rosaire, the chapel decorated by Matisse.

I lit a cigarette and tried to calm myself by contemplating the objects near at hand. Although I wouldn't admit it, I was in a fever of anticipation: after all, I had travelled more than six hundred miles for the sake of this meeting.

I had already spent one day in Vence – Vence-la-Jolie, as the inhabitants call it – the little Provençal town at the foot of the Baous Mountains, in which Matisse and Dufy had lived and painted, whose praises had been sung by Gide and Valéry, and where D. H. Lawrence met his tragic death.

I had already made some friends in this town, people who knew Chagall: the woman in the stationer's shop where he bought his papers, the master potter who helped him with the firing of his ceramics, the Mayor's German-speaking senior assistant, an Alsatian, who told me of the scheme for a Chagall Museum, for whose walls the Master was even now preparing designs.

The road that ran past me in a wide arc was the busy Avenue Henri Matisse. Even at this time of day, there was no break in the stream of cars. I had been able to see the road from my hotel window, and the vineyards, peach orchards and olive groves that surrounded it. The rocky peak above it was once painted by Poussin. From a distance the white and pink villas looked like toy bricks, and it was not easy to imagine that in one of these houses a magician painted pictures that mirrored the depth and brilliance of the universe.

I knew the dates and the circumstances under which most of his works had come into being. I knew Chagall's appearance from many descriptions and photographs. And yet I was doubtful whether the picture I had formed of the aspect and demeanour of Chagall the man really resembled what I was about to see. – After a little while I rose to my feet. When I stepped into the sun-flooded road I had the feeling that the air was completely still. There was a scent of jasmine, roses and wood fires. Had the strong French cigarette made me a trifle stupefied? Without meaning to, I took a few steps to where a gap between two houses opened out on to the panorama of the fortress-like Old Town of Vence shimmering in the midday sunlight. In a garden beside me hung purple-golden peaches nesting in silky green leaves, their colours as transparent as if they had been painted by Cézanne. Here nature automatically assumes the forms of the future work of art.

The little bell of the Chapel struck three high-pitched, vibrating strokes. A few instants later a deeper bell replied from the distant Cathedral tower. I turned round, went through the gate, and walked slowly up the drive to Chagall's house. The park ended at a further walled terrace, where carefully tended lawns and flowerbeds were visible between tall cedars and mighty palm trees. Now the whitewashed house gleamed quite close. The high, pistachio-green shutters were closed. The little side-building served as a garage, whose great doors stood wide open. Above it was the studio, with two big, white-curtained windows. Joined on to the right side of the house was a roofed terrace. Here a man was doing repairs. A large drawing had been scratched in the smooth plaster of the wall: a female figure and an animal that was at once a donkey, a horse and a cow. The strong light made the groove of the outline stand out clearly. The drawing looked like a relief, white in white with lilac shadows – an unusual Chagall.

A flight of steps led up to the door on the left side of the house, framed by the trailers and blossoms of red roses. Here, too, the door stood ajar. I pressed the bell, but heard no sound from within the house. The noise of the cars, which were still rushing past, further away now but in the same rhythm, was softened as though through a filter. Suddenly I heard once more the song of the cicadas that are to be found wherever cedars grow. No one came from the house, which seemed to be drowned in the noontide stillness. When a second peal of the bell failed to produce any sign of life, I walked round the house in search of the workman and told him my predicament.

I was on the point of going back to the door, when Madame Chagall came towards me and asked me, in German, to sit down on a garden seat made of wrought iron-wire in the shadow of the palms. Chagall appeared the same instant. It was evident that he had come from his studio; his short-sleeved, blue and yellow checked shirt and coarse, dark linen trousers showed traces of paint. The fingers of his right hand gleamed with minium. The painter wore an absent-minded look, as though he had just been giving all his attention to his work and could not yet focus it on a new object, the visitor. For a man living in the south, his face was strikingly pale, the green shadows of the trees made it look very flat. In the photographs I had seen his expression was somehow diabolic, rather like a character from one of E. T. A. Hoffmann's novels. The face of the man before me looked serious and a trifle weary. But the features came to life as Chagall began to talk. He spoke French fast, in a resonant, slightly lilting voice, making his statements rather shyly. He asked where I had come from, whether I had seen the Hanover exhibition, and how his paintings had been received by the Germans.

I told him I was not the only one upon whom this exhibition had had an overwhelming effect. Everywhere people were prophesying that modern painting had reached the limits of its potentialities, that it had run into a blind alley. But this exhibition had proved that the creations of modern painting represented a legitimate continuation of painting as such. It had brought the poetic core of painting into view again – the potential diversity and depth of artistic expression, and the human, animate element, which the young painters had failed to achieve in abstract painting, under whose spell they had grown up.
Chagall made a deprecating gesture. 'I don't know whether my pictures are good', he said quietly, 'I have no ambition to be modern. Abstract and non-abstract are no criteria for me. To my mind there is only good, authentic painting and – the opposite. Every thing else is unimportant. Good, honest painting is what I try to achieve. You are concerned with the problem of painting. Perhaps you can judge whether my pictures are good. I can't...' Chagall drew back his lips so that his clenched teeth showed. A brief grimace that reminded me of Charlie Chaplin's face in *Limelight*. 'I believe that time is an important factor in art, perhaps the most important. Works of art are sanctioned by time and not by people.'
I pointed out that his pictures in the Hanover exhibition showed to a high degree the *valeurs plastiques,* those elements of form and colour that are rarely treated as standards of judgement in the realm of German painting.
Chagall's eyes sought something present, some object in the immediate vicinity, with the aid of which he could explain something to me. 'The plastic values', he said, 'that's what matters. It took me more than forty years to grasp what the plastic values of a painting are – when the colours begin to sing. I felt it for the first time in Paris, in 1911. That was when I experienced light. I felt quite small, and there above', he gestured towards the sky ablaze with sunshine, 'was greatness, the fullness of light, Parnassus.'

Chagall paused and pulled his chair closer to the garden table. 'The greatest miracle is matter', he went on, 'not the physicist's matter that can be weighed and expressed in numbers and formulas. I mean the matter through which nature presents and expresses itself.'
Chagall pointed to a nearby tree. 'Look, that's what I mean by matter. You can see and hear it, it's full of form and colour and – life. It produces and radiates life. And then the greenery – *la verdure* . . . The painter has to try and get that into his painting. Paint too has its life, its mystery, its meaning – just like this matter – and the painter must study it, experience it, feel it . . . Everyone has a voice, but only a few can sing.' Chagall held the fingers of his left hand to his throat, as though to show where the voice was formed.
'I don't mean matter as surface, as the realists saw and represented it', he continued fervently. He pointed to an uncut stone sunk in the path, then drew his hand across the marble-top. 'That stone is living matter, full of *valeurs plastiques,* if I put my hand on it I can feel its pulsating life. But the table-top has been cut and polished by a machine, that's not matter, it's dead, it's nothing... *comprenez-vous?*' He flashed a glance at me out of the corner of his eye. 'The Impressionists saw only the surface, so did the Cubists, in spite of their tricks and their wallpaper patterns. A surface can be copied, but matter must be fashioned, it has life and sensibility, it's abstract and concrete at the same time, real and irreal.'
'Matter and plastic values', I continued after a pause – in Chagall's presence one could stay silent and think over what had been said – 'are intimately connected. You spoke just now about the "chemistry of colours", about the colour's own life. I think now of the example of the medieval painter, who was not yet conscious of being an artist, of the fact that what he was creating was art, creative expression with laws of its own. Nevertheless, his works prove that he was perfectly clear about what we call *valeurs plastiques,* that he consciously fashioned them. Don't you think that the holiness of the subject compelled the best of them to make matter "sing", as you put it?'
Chagall tilted his head back as though seeking an answer in the heraldically scalloped greenery of the palm fronds above us. He placed his arm behind the chair-back to support the upper part of his body, which was leaning over to one side. The movements of his body and hands seemed to adapt themselves to those of his thoughts and mental images. Now, as he began to answer, he leaned forward and placed his hands on the table-top. 'Every passion, every ecstasy can lend wings to the creative process and impel it forward', he replied. 'Perhaps they are necessary, *obligatoires...* There were good and bad painters even then. The difference did not lie in their piety, but in their painterly ability. The icon painters already used patterns; only the geniuses distinguished themselves by

their originality. It's just the same today. Most painters use patterns and tricks provided for them by the "isms". Shoe factories use patterns, they produce standardized factory work...' Chagall smiled roguishly. 'The handicraftsman, who is an artist, makes shoes to measure.' He pointed to my summer sandals. 'Les souliers de qualité, n'est-ce pas?'

Was Chagall trying to avoid the issue? I, too, had to laugh. But the question was so much on my mind that I asked it again. 'There is no such thing as "painterly ability" *per se*', I declared. 'That would be empty virtuosity. The comprehension and mastery of "painterly material", of "plastic values", presupposes something else – the participation of the heart, the soul, the whole inner man. Grünewald "knew what matter was all about". The putrefying body of Christ on the Isenheim Altar is matter brutally seen and brutally fashioned, and yet it expresses the very opposite of everything material, it expresses spirit, soul, pain and perhaps even divinity.'

'Rembrandt, Masaccio, Grünewald', enumerated Chagall, 'and perhaps Grünewald is the greatest. Of course matter cannot express itself, as the advocates of "automatism" believe. I was speaking of formed and transformed matter, of the voice that has become music. It is always filled with the spirit of whoever formed it, and if you meet it in this way it is also filled with another spirit of which the painter cannot speak and which enters it without his intervention. I have tried to bring my life and my pictures into harmony. My life is work, I only know work. I have few friends. I am still trying to put my ideas about painting into practice; I am not at all sure whether I succeed. The interest people take in my pictures always amazes me.'

At these words I thought of the intent faces of the young people in front of his pictures in the Hanover exhibition. Were they not all his friends and admirers? Must he not, as an artist, reckon with the receptiveness of the spectator? Does not the real effect of the work of art take place in the meeting between picture and spectator?

A cat crept past Chagall's chair, a noble animal with silver-grey fur flecked with white, and glittering blue eyes. It suddenly struck me how blue Chagall's eyes were. He lifted the animal up carefully and pressed it to his breast, holding and protecting it with both hands like something very precious, and spoke to it lovingly.

What I grasped at that moment was the earthly reality of Chagall the man, whose personality was extraordinary and full of riddles, and yet remained human in all its reactions. Confronted by his pictures I was inclined to think of the painter as transfigured into a character of legend. The correction of this idea simultaneously provided an answer to the question of whether his art was justified in our day and age. I believe that from this hour I saw Chagall's pictures as more 'earthly', but his 'earthliness' had acquired a new content, a deeper meaning, as had the whole reality of our existence.

My meeting with Chagall had lasted an hour. It took me days to extract the full value from the experience. It was not so much his words that I turned over in my mind. I was moved by the insight derived from seeing his various forms of expression as a whole, by the unity of man and artist, of the life and work of a painter in our time. Here no chasm yawned between existence and utterance, the mythical was not divorced from everyday life. The concept of reality was restored to its appropriate domain, to the realm of active forces created with tools. In Chagall's mouth, the word 'work' was divested of its distressing character and elevated to a creative existential act. The voice from within and the injunction from above had become identical. The conclusion drawn from it was not set before man as a categorical imperative, but as a gift, as a thank-offering to life.

The part played by the landscape of the South, of Provence, in the discovery of colour and the *valeurs plastiques* – for the recognition of which both Cézanne and van Gogh had striven, each according to his purpose – had become clear to me. 'There are places over which the spirit hovers', Barrès had said; here one felt its *douceur biblique,* its 'biblical sweetness', simply through the act of looking. The view through the open door of my hotel room on to the fruitful valley of Vence allowed me to gain a full appreciation of Chagall's expression 'the mystery of matter', and of that 'magical identity' between the works of nature and the artist, of which Maritain speaks.

Since the manifestations I saw and felt tangibly before me day and night were living, silently active nature, I had no need to try and reduce their meaning and character to a formula that could be introduced as required into the equation of art and life. The revelations that appeared to one here were more like those we gain from the silent presence of a beloved person: consciousness, like its dreaming counterpart, becomes imperceptibly filled with content without the observer feeling any necessity to arrange, apply or question his experience. I needed only to enumerate what offered itself to my eyes and senses. The appeal of things, phenomena and beings included that other element, their mystery. Seen with the painter's eye, this reality expressed itself as colour, of which Cézanne – looking at the same landscape – said that it was 'capable of expressing more truth than the factual characteristics of a model', that is to say of any phenomenon.

In the stillness and solitude of the following days I came to put a different interpretation on many of Chagall's words. Had I not sought to contradict him when he told me that he did not work for people? It was probably no coincidence that I came just then upon a passage in Maritain's critical studies that supplemented

Chagall's statement. During our conversation I had already felt that my unspoken objection regarding the 'active participation of the spectator', without which the work of art does not unfold its fullest potentialities, was invalid, despite the specious cogency with which it had presented itself during the discussion.

'The artist does not produce his work for people', it says in Maritain, 'or at most for future generations, whom he imagines in a sense as unreal, because not yet existent. It is not his wish to be understood, but to live on in history.' This sentence gave quite a new significance to the concept of time, of which Chagall had spoken. 'The artist', Maritain goes on, 'would suffer even more deeply if the public understood him; for then he has to ask himself whether his work does not lack that extra something which, if it were understood, could not have been communicated.'

Could the artist withdraw into solitude and yet say, as Chagall said, that he was seeking love? Had I not striven to find out how much effective creative activity and the urge to inner communication mutually determine one another? Here again I found the answer in Maritain, Chagall's friend. Perhaps the painter's example had inspired the philospher and poet to write:

'The creative is formed in the substance of the soul at various levels, and through this fact everyone reveals what he has in him; the greater a poet is, the deeper the plane of creative vision sinks into the densest being of his soul. At the same time, however, the simpler the poet becomes, the more willingly he casts aside every mask, the readier he is to say what he is, the more strongly he feels the value of human community. The whole problem for the artist consists in having, along with greater technical skill, which can be learnt, a deep soul, which cannot be learnt. Even pain does not suffice for this.'

It was at almost the same time in the afternoon, a few days later, that I stood once more in front of the white house. For an instant I saw before me the faded photograph from the glass-case in the Musée d'Art Moderne in Paris, the photograph of the simple, dark wooden house in Vitebsk, with its crooked shutters, in which Chagall was born. There was no garden, no green leaves, no flowers. What a contrast to the aristocratic park and the villa in the style of J. J. Rousseau, fringed by the palms of the Côte d'Azur.

Again it was Madame Chagall who greeted me. She did not treat me like a visitor who had come to her house for only the second time, but asked me to go inside and look round, while she went to fetch Marc.

I was alone in the dusky hall. The doors of the rooms stood open. In spite of the closed shutters, they were lighter than I had expected. On the right a drawing room opened on to the garden. It contained little furniture. Above the marble fireplace hung the great square picture with the soaring lovers, the cock and the Eiffel Tower. Its colours were those of the room: a ghostly, solemn white, a shimmering emerald and a transparent cobalt with violet shadows. Alongside a small Maillol sculpture, on a low circular table in front of the tall French windows, blossomed roses, whose scent I imagined I could smell out here in the hall. If the creative vision has its origin in the 'night-side of consciousness', then the scene of which I was the astonished spectator resembled the state of the picture before its birth. I had already seen the work in an exhibition. But how much more mysteriously it shone forth at this place and at this hour!

On the mantlepiece a light-coloured, gay earthenware figure by Henri Laurens squatted in front of a large oval ceramic plate by Chagall. The nude shimmering from the indigo glaze was like the magical reflection of the sculpture.

On the left opened a bright cosy-looking room. I looked at a window with white muslin curtains and a book-case in spruce, filled with French books. On the bookshelf, leaning against the wall, stood a large earthenware tile bearing a head of Christ. The colours and shapes of the face might have come from El Greco. Since Chagall had painted them they were both sadder and milder.

I walked over to a glass case in the farthest corner of the hall that contained a whole collection of Chagall's ceramics. As I looked at them I could not help thinking of the Picasso ceramics I had seen a few days earlier in the Grimaldi Museum in Antibes, in those huge rooms, flooded by the light of the sea, which open on to the most grandiose marine view known to painting – two corresponding blues separated by the almost invisible seam of the horizon. Those fauns, Silenuses, nereids, centaurs and girls' bodies, graceful or swollen like Demeter, drawn with the sensibility of a Greek vase painter – touched in with Impressionist dots, or incised with the sweeping strokes of sudden impulse – could live only in and by this abundance of light. They were recognizable from a distance, their relationship to the Celto-Ligurian sculpture in the lower rooms of the Museum seemed as evident as their affinity with the contemporary colourfulness of the sun-tanned youths and lasciviously charming girls against the background of Antibes Lido with the Tricolour flying overhead.

I had to go close up to Chagall's ceramics; the colours and outlines, the brilliance and liveliness of the glaze only became clear when the eyes explored them. This was not the triumphant vitality of an artist in whose brilliantly skilled hands every material was transformed into a cogent metaphor. Here a poet listened for the revelations of the struggle between fire and earth, and watched in amazement the metamorphoses his ever new, and yet old, world of images underwent in this new, and yet old, material. Here every nuance of colour, every movement of the surface corresponded to the stirrings of devout

Portrait of the artist by Maywald, Paris

emotion; and yet the earth remained earth and the pigment combined with the earth to form a truer concept of matter. Here the lover and the beloved emerged from a vibrant background, and yet remained one with the emerald green, the well-blue and the gold of the stars that arched above them. This was the other world that the South gives to men, the *douceur biblique* of the *Songs of Songs*. These thoughts passed through my mind during the few seconds of waiting; I had not noticed that another spectator had come silently to my side – Chagall himself. He greeted me with an animated gesture. He seemed more relaxed and friendly than at our first meeting. This time he wore over his checked shirt a blue linen jacket, which made his figure seem more slender and at the same time tauter. Now I could see how thin his curly white hair was. His pale blue eyes lay under full lids. Between his bushy eyebrows a wrinkle ran up into his forehead, which lost its severity when Chagall raised his brows. Then his forehead was enlivened by a multitude of folds, and the leathery skin of his cheeks crinkled up. The bridge of his nose was strong and arched, giving his face a birdlike look. But there was nothing aggressive about its expression: the deep furrows running from the fleshy nostrils to the corners of the mouth lent the face, however relaxed it might appear, an introspective, even melancholy, look.

I had less time for my observations than I have used words to describe them. Chagall was animated and quickly changed the subject of his speech and actions. He switched on the light in the glass case, and the same moment he seemed to laugh about it. He pointed first to one then to another piece of pottery. 'I often feel I'd like to do something else than paint for a change, but everything comes back to painting in the end. But I like handling clay. It's the most delicate of all materials. I like to be close to the earth.' With the fingers of his right hand he stroked the inside of a brown-glazed plate, which he had taken from a hall table, simultaneously feeling it and drawing my attention to it. From the iridescent glaze there appeared the figures of two girls and the green and red of leaves and flowers touched lightly in. 'Is there anything more mysterious than earth and flowers?' he asked. 'At the same time, everything must remain a unity, in the work of art as in nature. That's what the landscape here teaches me.'

He put the plate back and went with me into the smaller room. His attitude was less that of the master of the house than of a man showing a guest the sights in a friend's house, in which he himself is still a stranger. Now he pointed to the tile with the head of Christ. 'It's an experiment', he explained. 'I should like to make a mural in pottery. Religious, in the sense of my illustrations for the Bible. Not decorative – but pure painting, painting on clay, the material of this landscape. I cannot imagine Christ from the point of view of a creed or a dogma. My picture of Christ is intended to be human, full of love and sorrow. I don't want to stress the religious element: art, painting is religious by nature –

like everything creative. What interests me in designing a picture is its construction. It has its logic, hasn't it? And yet you can't paint a picture with logic. It's the same with religion and dogma, with poetry and rules. Dogma means separation; and separation means conflict, struggle, hate and war.'
As we passed the picture hanging over the fireplace I stopped, in the hope that Chagall would say something about it. But he only smiled, as the old pianist Cortot used to smile when he played a passage of which he was particularly fond. 'That's the ardent love of the young, the poets sing about', I said – it was more of a question than a statement. 'Love has its stages, one form of love secretly prepares the way for another. First the human being is the adored object, the lovers clasp one another, they soar over roofs and countries. The beasts of the earth and the angels accompany them. But finally, love of a human being is only an intermediary that allows us to catch a glimpse of the other dimension, that of the greater love which Christ meant, the Christ you paint, the Christ you have so often painted. Even your figures of Christ have changed, they have become more and more majestic, more spiritual, more kindly and – sadder.'
Chagall did not answer. On the little round table lay a book of reproductions of the 19th century paintings in the possession of the Louvre. It had just arrived; a Paris publisher had sent it to Chagall. He picked it up and turned the pages. A picture by Daumier, van Gogh's *Landscape with Stars*, Cézanne's great fragment *The Bathers*. At every picture Chagall nodded approvingly and – reverently. 'Everyone says it in his own way, but especially in the language of painting', said Chagall finally, 'and they all mean the same thing: Christ, the great love, the nobly human. Not as a theme, only as painting ... If I have painted Christ it came about solely through painting, through the brush on the canvas. Perhaps it was necessary, for the picture – or for me, who can say. It's not something you can talk about. But one thing I know, I can't produce religious art, programme art – no, that would be dreadful.'
Chagall had turned the leaves of the book; the first picture appeared last – David's *Napoleon*. '... like this, art for the reading-book, I could never have done it.' He put the book down on the table, unwillingly and yet smiling again. He glanced into the adjoining room. Madame Chagall had laid a tea table under the great *Wedding* picture of 1910. Chagall took my arm and led me to the other guests in the room. 'I've been talking too much', he said as though apologetically to his wife, and suddenly the old roguishness sparkled out of the corner of his eye. 'Is he going to write it all down?' As he said this he made a gesture with his hand, imitating a man busily writing.
I repeated what I had said to Chagall at the beginning: that a word – especially when it is spoken to the young – can open doors. This task would be looked on by many as unimportant, but it meant a great deal to me.

'It is a good thing to open doors', Chagall broke in. 'What else am I trying to do? They are all tiny efforts, yours and mine. But together – and other people's efforts with them – they add up to something; we can't hope for more than that.'

In the Musée d'Art Moderne

How Chagall lives, works and thinks nowadays I had been able to find out at Vence-la-Jolie. To understand his human and artistic evolution, and thereby the peculiar quality of his whole work, I had to let the other stages on his road enter my consciousness, I had to prepare myself to follow the complex stratification of meaning that can be felt in every one of his works, his tensions and condensations, and to share in the wealth and depth of his revelations.
For most visitors the way to Vence runs via Paris. This was also true of the painter, who did not make up his mind to seek the light and warmth of Provence – under whose influence his pictures, like the fruit of this landscape, gained their final ripeness – until he had spent some time in Paris, where his art developed and grew firm.
The traveller, too, may become aware that Paris is more than a mere geographical stage on the way to the South. It was so with me. The moment my eyes once more absorbed the light of this city, the moment I breathed its atmosphere laden with all kinds of tensions and heard once more the diction of its inhabitants' language, I straight away discovered a link with the centre of my interests – Chagall.

Wherever I found myself in this city of millions, its great landmark towered up into the blue of a cloudless sky. It was the same Eiffel Tower celebrated in many of Chagall's pictures, the eloquent witness of a life permeated with love and artistic fervour, the focal point of Paris – the metropolis that has changed with the passing years and the changing destinies of nations, and yet remained fundamentally the same.
There was no better opportunity of seeing Chagall's pictures and studying this painter in the proximity of other members of the 'Ecole de Paris' than in the Museum of Modern Art, next to the Palais de Chaillot. The life that revealed itself in the many streets and side-streets on the way to and from the Museum – the children playing in the sunny roadways through the park, the loving couples kissing unabashed, the squares, quays and terraces – seemed to prelude the artistic revelations awaiting me in the Museum, and on the way back to confirm them.

The life I had experienced became a memory as soon as I took my eyes off the phenomena that had just been delighting me. In the pictures in the Museum, however, I saw the immediacy of experience fixed in the permanency of the work of art. The sensations of colour, movement and *joie de vivre* that had so gripped me on my way to these pictures now radiated, in transmuted shape, from the hundreds of masterpieces which, despite their youth, constitute part of the glory of French art.

It has been asked why painting seems predestined to represent happiness, indeed to *be* happiness. I do not mean the happiness of artistic realization, that fleeting and yet precise instant that never ceases to bring happiness to those who possess the sensibility to receive its boon – this kind of happiness is contained in every artistic creation, no matter how tragic its content. I mean, rather, happiness seen and treated as subject matter – a thing that appears so unfitting to contemporary literature. This happiness is contained in the very paint itself as material and radiation; and the paint compels the painter to lavish it on the canvas, to wipe its materiality from memory, to make it sing. Painting therefore involves elevating the life that has been experienced to the level of poetry, which is its true determinant and source.

It may have been a coincidence that, at the time when I visited the Museum, the works were arranged in such a way that I had to pass through all the rooms to reach the one containing Chagall's paintings. Thus I could not fail also to take a look at the other rooms, in which the works of the Neo-Impressionists, Nabis, Fauves, Cubists, Surrealists and Tachistes or 'action painters' were hung. I spent some time in each room, recalling the significance which this, that or the other picture possessed for me. The various chambers of my consciousness were capable of being filled up by one or other of them, just as I was able at various times to enjoy Bach or Schumann with the same enthusiasm and the same inner profit. This alternation of interest caused me to make new discoveries even in what was familiar to me.

These discoveries were also always self-discoveries – in line with Goethe's dictum that the things we see awaken a new organ in us. Moreover, I gained a direct experience of the phenomenon of history: for every painter filled the space and the fragment of time allotted him. 'Every great man is engaged on a mission, and history is the name of the inexplicable process in which one man of genius receives the mission from another and increases or diminishes it' (Felix Braun).

Matisse was the ever young in spirit. He enchants by his colours, the geometry of his forms, in which he carries the optically visible to the maximum pitch of intensity. 'Anything that is not expressible is not French', wrote Charles du Bos. In this sense Matisse is the most French of all painters. His pictures are feasts for

the eyes; his blues, greens, reds and yellows the notes of a delightful music that stirs and cheers us by creating, for a few moments, the illusion of perfect happiness. Any attempt to link his colours and forms with subjective feeling was bound, in his eyes, to disturb the unique harmony of his 'decorations'. None the less, the smile of his landscapes, flowers and women does not conceal the mystery of their ultimately mystical transformation; there is something sphinxlike about it, as in Leonardo. Matisse's later works often disclose an underlying shiver, despite the sparkle with which they are disguised.
Rouault, whose urge to artistic creation sprang from a deep religious sense, sought and in his own way found the mystic union with phenomena. This artist has been called the Léon Bloy of painting; in fact the glow of altar-paintings on a background of gold-leaf shines from his faces of Christ, his saints, his pictures of the insulted and humiliated. But there is something grimly accusing and eruptive about his creations, something alien to the ikons. Their dogmatic zeal threatens to burst out of the realm of poetry.
Finally, Picasso represents the passionate concentration of everything still possible and permitted in art, a disclosure of the functions with whose aid phenomena, and with them man, who identifies himself with them, attract and repel one another; sceptically and yet full of creative triumph, the constellations of the visible world are discovered and intensified into mighty metaphors; here the knife-sharp seam is reached that joins together painterly subtlety and barbaric passion, leaving the spectator uncertain whether it is the laughter of Pan or the smile of Satan the seducer that springs and sings from his pictures.
Chagall shares with Picasso a rebellious and compulsive quality. But when his voice becomes audible in the choir of the moderns, it is as though a breath from another world were wafted towards us. In his work the hymn to life has found its most poignant expression.

'Churches, Fences, Shops, Synagogues...'

No visitor to the Musée d'Art Moderne will fail to look at the low glass case in the Chagall room in which photographs from the life of this painter lie spread out.
One of these photographs, yellow with age, shows the house in which Chagall was born: a narrow path paved with headstones leads to a single-storey building of planks, whose walls threaten to fall forward. Shutters hang crookedly beside the dark holes of the windows. The roof is covered with shingles. In the street stand peasant women with headscarves and two men in Russian blouses and peaked caps.

The picture of this house, this street corner, and of Vitebsk as a whole with its market-place, its thirty odd churches, its synagogues, its cemetery, and its bridges, was to be conjured up in many of Chagall's paintings, more insistently with each one.

On a card in the glass case we read that Marc Chagall was born on July 7, 1887, in Vitebsk, the district capital of the province of the same name on the Russo-Polish border. Vitebsk, which lay on both sides of the Dvina, had at that time sixty-thousand inhabitants, of whom almost half were Jews.

Biographies always begin with place-names and dates. The reader rarely pays much heed to them; he hardly expects to meet them again on later pages. The life of the German painter August Macke, a man of the same age as Chagall, begins with the words: 'He was born at Meschede, which played no further role in his life.'

In Chagall's case, however, the name Vitebsk and all the lived and dreamed reality contained in it, were of overwhelming significance. For Chagall Vitebsk was not only his place of origin, but also his present and his goal. For Chagall the painter and poet it is self-evident that the trinity of space, time and life is revealed as 'real' – that is to say, operative – only in the unity of the work of art. Whatever Chagall may experience and create, whatever subjects he may choose for his paintings, however many people he meets and wherever his travels may take him, all this will be dominated by the recollection of his childhood impressions.

There is also a photograph of his parents, taken on their wedding day. The young bridegroom, in a long caftan-like coat with a peaked cap on his head, is sitting by a small table with carved legs. Beside him, her hand resting on an upholstered chair-back and only slightly overtopping the sitting man, stands the dainty bride in a close-fitting black silk costume with many ruches and ribbons.

As Chagall relates, his father used to rise at six every morning and go to the synagogue before work. Chagall's paternal grandfather was a *melamed*, a teacher of religion; his mother's father was a *shochet*, a master butcher, who spent half his day praying and studying the sacred books in the synagogue. The whole family – Chagall had eight sisters and one brother, while half a dozen uncles and aunts lived in Vitebsk alone – were ardent Chassidim, members of the popular religious movement that sprang to life among the Polish Jews and strove to counter the severity and asceticism of the Talmud by rendering religious life deeper and more sincere.

'When I first opened my eyes', wrote Chagall later, 'I met a world, of the town, of the house, that took a gradual and lasting hold on me.' He relates how his mother told him that on the night he was born the Jewish quarter of Vitebsk was in flames. 'They took the bed and the mattress, the mother and the child at her feet, and carried them to a safer place in another part of the town.' Impressions like these also left their mark in Chagall's memory.

Chagall has always considered himself a son of the people; he believed that this was the most sensitive section of the population. So we must imagine the young Marc as a sensitive lad, quick of hearing, a dreamer always surprised and wonderstruck in this reality of the Jewish ghetto, peasant simplicity and pious family life. In spite of persecution and oppression, these Jews had not ceased to praise God, whom – according to the Chassidic doctrine – they believed to be embodied and present in every manifestation of life on earth.

Marc saw the reality of his environment as no one else did; he looked at it in the magic of its essential being, and not at the potential practical utility it might have for his own development. 'All around were churches, fences, shops and synagogues', he relates, 'simple, monosyllabic and eternal like the buildings on Giotto's frescoes. All round me, this way and that, weave and wind and walk Jews of all sorts and all ages, Tems from Javitch and Tems from Belin. A beggar hurries home, a rich man walks home. A boy from the *Cheder* goes home. Father goes home. There were no cinemas in those days. Everyone went home or into the shops...'

At the age of thirteen Marc, who had meanwhile 'tasted the intoxication of drawing', was supposed to be apprenticed to a trader, so that he might one day become a merchant, and not a mere workman like his father. But he showed neither inclination nor aptitude for this profession, and he was allowed to remain another four years at school. Then one day he surprised his parents by his wish to become a painter. He had learnt that there was an art school in Vitebsk run by a painter named Judah Pen. With his mother's support, he succeeded in getting into this school. But after three months he could stand it no longer.

Young Chagall's artistic gifts were as original and naive as a child's. His artistic development was not subject to the fatal destiny to which most artistically minded children are exposed. It ran on without a break, through and beyond puberty, and expanded and deepened in pace with his spiritual and human maturity. Chagall never experienced the discrepancy between natural gifts and academic compulsion, and the resulting uncertainties and disturbances, that occur in almost every artistic individual. It is no doubt due to this fact that academic instruction left him as unsatisfied as schools and 'isms' did later.

His parents sent him for a short time as apprentice to a photographer, in the belief that he might derive some satisfaction from this occupation. But the darkroom appealed to him even less than the art school. He wanted to paint pictures, not to retouch photographic plates.

1 *The Sabbath, 1909*

A friend with whom he used to roam the countryside drawing and painting on Sundays advised him to go to the Imperial Academy of Art at St Petersburg. The Tzarist laws were very strict. No Jew was allowed to live in the capital unless he exercised a profession that justified his residence there. So Chagall officially acted as business representative for the merchants of Vitebsk. Another difficulty lay in the fact that the minimum age at which students were accepted in the Academy was eighteen. Since Chagall was only sixteen at that time, his father changed the date on his birth certificate. With only 27 roubles in his pocket – his father could give him no more – he set out for the brilliant great city on the Neva.

St Petersburg

At this period St Petersburg boasted an artistic life equal to that of any other European metropolis. Russian music, literature, theatre and ballet were in their heyday; the fame of Russian theatrical producers went beyond the national frontiers. The ballet, under its Maecenas and impressario Serge Diaghilev, gave immensely successful performances in almost every European capital. Diaghilev, who himself showed talent as a painter, had the knack of harnessing the most important dancers, painters and composers of the Old World to his artistic enthusiasm.

Painting, on the other hand, had proved incapable of rising above academic provincialism; it lacked independence and wavered between realistic historical painting, a forced archaicism, playful imitation of rococo in the style of Alexander I, and mawkish representation. And yet the painters working in St Petersburg had an opportunity of studying the outstanding representatives of European painting in the Hermitage, which possessed thirty paintings by Rembrandt alone. Moreover, there were at this time in the city of the Neva, according to the estimate of Lunacharsky, who later became People's Commissar, three hundred private collections, where even pictures by Picasso, Matisse and Modigliani could be seen.

'The Russian painters', wrote Burlyuk, a critic of the period, 'were distinguished by a terrified laziness – they all suffered from Oblomov's disease, and in this respect they were truly national.' The Belgian poet Verhaeren, who won fame as the extoller and interpreter of the young French art, is said to have shrugged his shoulders in embarrassment during a visit to a St Petersburg gallery; while the modest and excessively courteous painter Maurice Denis 'wore a crooked smile' as he walked through an exhibition of Russian painting organized in Paris by Diaghilev.

And yet the artists who thronged round this Maecenas and gave their group the name of the periodical he published, *Mir Iskusstva,* The World of Art, were full of revolutionary élan. These artists, Somoff, Syeroff, Golovin, Benois and above all Bakst, were striving for a form of art corresponding to French Impressionism and defended the thesis *L'art pour l'art,* to which – in contradistinction to the Imperial Academy of Art – official Russia subscribed. In 1905 the Imperial Puppet Theatre in St Petersburg commissioned Bakst to design the décor for a ballet, which introduced a new era in modern stage scenery. It seems almost a joke to recall that this piece was Bayer's Die Puppenfee *(The Doll Fairy).*

The later Communist writer Alexis Tolstoy wrote of the climate prevailing in the modernist camp at this period: 'I well remember how we waited for the end of the world in 1910: the tail of Halley's comet was expected to come into contact with the earth and fill the whole atmosphere with deadly gases in an instant. The whole of Russian art, from top to bottom, lived in dull foreboding of destruction and was one single cry of deathly boredom. The last generation of the "Fishers of Eternity" fell into a state of frenzy and horror. People soiled their faces with filthy scribbles, they stood on their heads and shouted, "The whole world's standing on its head".'
Marinetti delivered a lecture on Futurism in St Petersburg; his revolutionary theses and prognoses were enthusiastically taken up by the young *avant-garde.* The poet Mayakovsky, who later became the Expressionist spokesman of Communist lyric poetry and then put a bullet through his brain, called the atmosphere in Russia at this time 'as sinister as daggers and feverish as a violent illness'.

For Chagall, his stay in St Petersburg began with a disappointment: he failed the entrance examination for Baron von Stieglitz's Academy. In order not to lose his right to stay in the city, he went to the school of the 'Society for the Protection of the Arts', where he even obtained a grant of ten roubles a month. This was supplemented by occasional assistance from well-wishers. He lived with working people and himself worked as manservant in the household of a lawyer. But the fact that he was a Jew gave him more trouble than his lack of money. After he had been thrown into prison for a few days because he had no labour permit, he made efforts to obtain a regular craftsman's patent, and apprenticed himself to a signwriter with the aim of obtaining the certificate of a craft school. But the prospect of sitting another examination did not appeal to him. He could, he tells us, 'paint a smoking Turk or fruit', but he was certain he could not pass the lettering test. Nevertheless, he set to work. At the same time he attended the 'Society for the Protection of the Arts'. But even here he

did not feel sure that what he was doing was really worth while. His first two years at St Petersburg seemed to have been wasted.
At last Chagall applied for admission to Bakst's art school, although the fees were thirty roubles a month – a considerable sum for the young painter, who had to earn the money by signwriting. Bakst accepted him. Chagall shared the studio with the dancer Nijinsky, who later became so famous, and Tolstoy's daughter Vera. Bakst, like the rest of the *Mir Iskusstva* painters, was a masterly draughtsman, a skilled imitator of styles; his secret model was the Renaissance. These qualities made him the outstanding theatrical designer of his age. Understandably, he left the young Chagall, who was impelled towards a more elemental use of artistic media, unsatisfied. So Chagall remained only a few months with Bakst. His artistic will at this period finds expression in a woman's head that shows how independently and confidently the seventeen-year-old lad could grasp and construct a piece of physiognomy. Forms and colours are audaciously condensed, in the manner of the Fauves. This study reveals where Chagall could still gain instruction and stimulus – in Paris!

But first he had to go back to Vitebsk. In a simple and familiar environment, young Chagall at least felt at home as a human being; and when he took out canvas, brushes and paint again, it became evident that he had meanwhile acquired an artistic outlook of his own, the necessary painterly technique, and a personal style. During the coming weeks he produced pictures in which the world of his future *œuvre* is already foreshadowed in subject-matter and expression.
They are of medium size and painted on coarse sacking, the paint being applied dry. His chromatic scale, which is low in tone, is made up of brown, ochre, a dull green and blue. These were the colours Chagall had observed as reflections on the phenomena in the immediate vicinity of his parents' house, where, as he tells us himself, there was little greenery and no flowers.
In these early pictures the people fill the spaces between the scenery of their wretched world. Their heads are over-large, their hands lie heavy and tired in their laps, on the arm of a child or of one of their fellows. These figures, who seem to be suffering existence rather than actively shaping it, muse over their life's dream, the open window allows the stillness of the room to flow out into the Sabbath peace of the village.
This silence is not the eerie echo that often represents the fruit of strenuous looking. These figures do not appear 'studied' in the optical sense; they seem to be the result of inward contemplation, of a memory, of a dream. The people in these quiet rooms lack the sentimental or even aggressive quality of 'paintings of the poor'; their pathos is nourished from other sources, sources an-

nounced by the subsequent pictures that have as their subjects marriage, birth and death.

Birth, Marriage, Death

In the painting *Birth* (1910) Chagall portrayed the turbulent activity in a peasant room, with the midwife holding the struggling, screaming child in her arms, the villagers crowding wide-eyed round the door together with the stupidly staring calf, and the father crawling out from under the bed, on which his wife, the chief character in the drama, lies like a supernumerary beneath a huge red canopy. The scene is immersed in the red light of a petrol lamp, which forms a strong contrast to the intense yellowish green of the background. Candles, lamps and lanterns occur in many of Chagall's paintings, even the later ones. In the Russian painter's work, as in van Gogh's, the way in which the source of light casts its beam is symbolic of the stage of his human and artistic development. The scale of light runs from a dramatic flare to a supernatural, gentle glow. In the pictures of this period the light is somehow disturbing and weird.

In the picture *Wedding* (1909) a village street rises to the upper edge of the picture, which simultaneously represents the horizon of the composition's landscape. A wedding procession comes down the street, a dozen people. Beside them stand a few onlookers. People are playing the fiddle, chattering, lamenting and staring. The noise of the shouting and gesticulating people seems to be drowned by a silence that renders all the voices unreal. Here again light is not lacking; this time it is the thin gleam of a streetlamp in the ghostly glimmer of dawn. This street appears to the spectator to be the world itself and the little group of people its inhabitants.

In the picture *Death* or *Candles in a Dark Street* (1908) we once more see a street. This time it leads from the whole width of the lower edge of the painting to the centre. It is indigo green in colour. A dead man lies along the street. The whitish yellow skull and the stiff, naked feet look out from beneath a red shroud. Round the dead man stand six candles burning with an orange-coloured flame. A woman laments with upstretched arms in the nocturnal silence of the village. Her blouse gleams poison green, her ankle-length skirt is ghostly white.

At the end of the street – without any perspective foreshortening – a street-sweeper (Death) bends over his broom. Peasant houses, pale pink in colour, cluster watchful and frightened along the edges of the street. With their crooked window-frames pushed into the corners, and their dangling shutters, they have more facial expression than the few people in the street.

From the gable of a house projects a shoemaker's sign – a boot. A man with a fiddle sits astride the roof, crouching dreamily over his instrument. The sky above, across which thin black clouds drift, glows with a fiery green.
This picture was regarded in every detail by Chagall as a reality. He relates that several different experiences are combined in it. He heard one night from his bedroom, which he shared with his brother, the cries of a woman waking the neighbours from their sleep with calls for help, because her husband lay dying. The following morning Chagall caught a glimpse of the dead man lying on the earthen floor of the passage of a house, surrounded by six candles.
The man on the roof is a recollection of an incident that occured during a family gathering. During the festive hubbub someone noticed that the grandfather was missing: he was found at last sitting on the roof of the low house, where he was consuming a dish of beetroot in peace and quiet, away from the noise of the relatives. Finally, the fiddle belonged to Chagall's Uncle Neuch, whom he admired above everything and who played this instrument 'like a cobbler'.
If imagination means the linking up of various elements of experience into a new complex of meaning, then the wealth and density of Chagall's imagination may be judged from this last picture. The significance of the painting goes beyond what can be put into a description of its contents; and yet the 'subject matter' is what gives life and depth to the purely painterly elements of the picture.
The young Chagall, however, is not confined within the phases of this particular cycle; he has other systems of notation at his disposal. A portrait of his sister is radiant with restrained colour; the expression of her face is drawn with great love and understanding. This portrait is more than a study of a model who happened to be available. The glowing colours of a red blouse and a bunch of flowers with deep blue blossoms call to mind those that were to appear in later works. There are other studies from this period in the artist's possession: oil sketches and drawings of his parents, brother and sisters, and relations. The preservation of these early productions might be taken for an understandable act of piety towards the testimonies to his own artistic beginnings. But seeing these studies all together, the spectator is struck by the extent to which they represent a record of devout family feeling. Sketches from the early periods of other painters generally reveal a multiplicity of themes that lack this dutiful community of meaning. But with Chagall the basis of his thought and feeling finds expression even in these studies. Thus his French biographer, Vladimir Weidlé, is probably right when he says: 'Marriage, procreation, motherhood, the feeling of belonging to the same nest, of being the son of the same father, is Chagall's essential theme; it has either a religious significance or none at all...'

The antithesis and wealth of Chagall's artistic means, which have already been pointed out, are nowhere more in evidence than in two pictures which no one would guess to have been painted by the same painter in the same year. The first, another scene in a peasant room, is entitled *Sabbath* (1909). In it we find all the attributes that are also characteristic of his later work.

Again there is a family in the room. Men are sitting on high-backed chairs round a table on which two candles and a petrol lamp are burning. A figure is leaning out of bed; a woman stands praying in the doorway. The window in the rear wall is curtained with a cloth; a burning lamp hangs from the ceiling; a clock with a weight and pendulum ticks on the wall. The figures, the furniture, the lamp – everything is individually perceived; the whole painting seems inspired by an overwhelming encounter that lends the composition unity within a new dimension of perception that is also proclaimed by the colouring. The colours raise everything into the domain of the marvellous, before which the figures' aspect of poverty loses all importance. A harsh lemon yellow rends the poison green shadows on the walls. Here the human figures do not fill the space, as in the earlier pictures, but are dominated by space, which bears down upon us and makes us fellow-participants in this portentous scene.
The second picture, the *Portrait of My Fiancée in Black Gloves* (1909), is a portrait of Bella, who became Chagall's wife and wise, magnanimous muse. In turning to classical portraiture Chagall shows the pride of the lover, who wishes to depict his beloved as nobly and beautifully as possible. Perhaps, in addition to this, he wanted to prove to the painters at St Petersburg that he could also paint pictures that would satisfy their demand for representation and tradition.

And yet this portrait is thoroughly 'Chagallian'. The slender, soft figure of the girl, the close-fitting sleeves of the white dress, the lace collar painted with all the care of Renoir, the elegant silhouette of the gloved hands are more than a purely painterly avowal. To celebrate his love for Bella through the medium of painting was to be for decades the mainspring of his life as man and artist.
Bella, who was six years younger than Marc and had been his friend since earliest childhood, was the daughter of a Vitebsk jeweller. She studied Russian literature and journalism in Moscow.
Great as was Chagall's urge to go to Paris, it was not so easy to make his way there from Vitebsk. How was he to find the money, how was he to earn a living when he first arrived in Paris? He had no alternative but first to return to St Petersburg.
This time he was more fortunate. He found a lawyer, Vinaver, a member of the Duma and leader of the Constitutional Democratic Party, who was a great lover of art. Vinaver recognized the special quality of his work and bought two paintings from him – the portrait of Bella and *The Wedding*. He found him a studio, treated him like a son, and finally made him an allowance to study abroad. Faced with the question of whether Rome or Paris offered the greatest advantages, Chagall chose Paris. 'The soil that nourished the roots of my art was Vitebsk', he confessed later. 'But my art desired Paris as a tree desires water. Otherwise it would have withered . . .'

Cubism

In the years before the First World War Paris was alive with new and audacious ideas. It was not only the capital of France, but the metropolis of the intellectual and artistic world, and it exercised a tremendous attraction on all those who longed for a renewal of artistic life.
All the names that today represent the spirit of contemporary art kept a rendezvous in Paris. We meet here, if only for a short space of time, August Macke and Paul Klee, Rilke and Ezra Pound. Many of the newcomers prolonged their visit into permanent residence, among them the Russians Stravinsky and Archipenko, Benois and Zadkine, the Italians Modigliani and Chirico, the Spaniards Picasso and Juan Gris, the Roumanian Pascin and the Pole Soutine. There was a German, a Scandinavian, a Russian and an American artists' colony, which met in the painting schools of Julian and Matisse, in the galleries on the Left Bank, and in the cafés of the Boulevard Saint-Michel.
What was it that made residence in Paris so attractive to these people? Was it the colourful life of its inhabitants, their endearing humanity? Was it the more

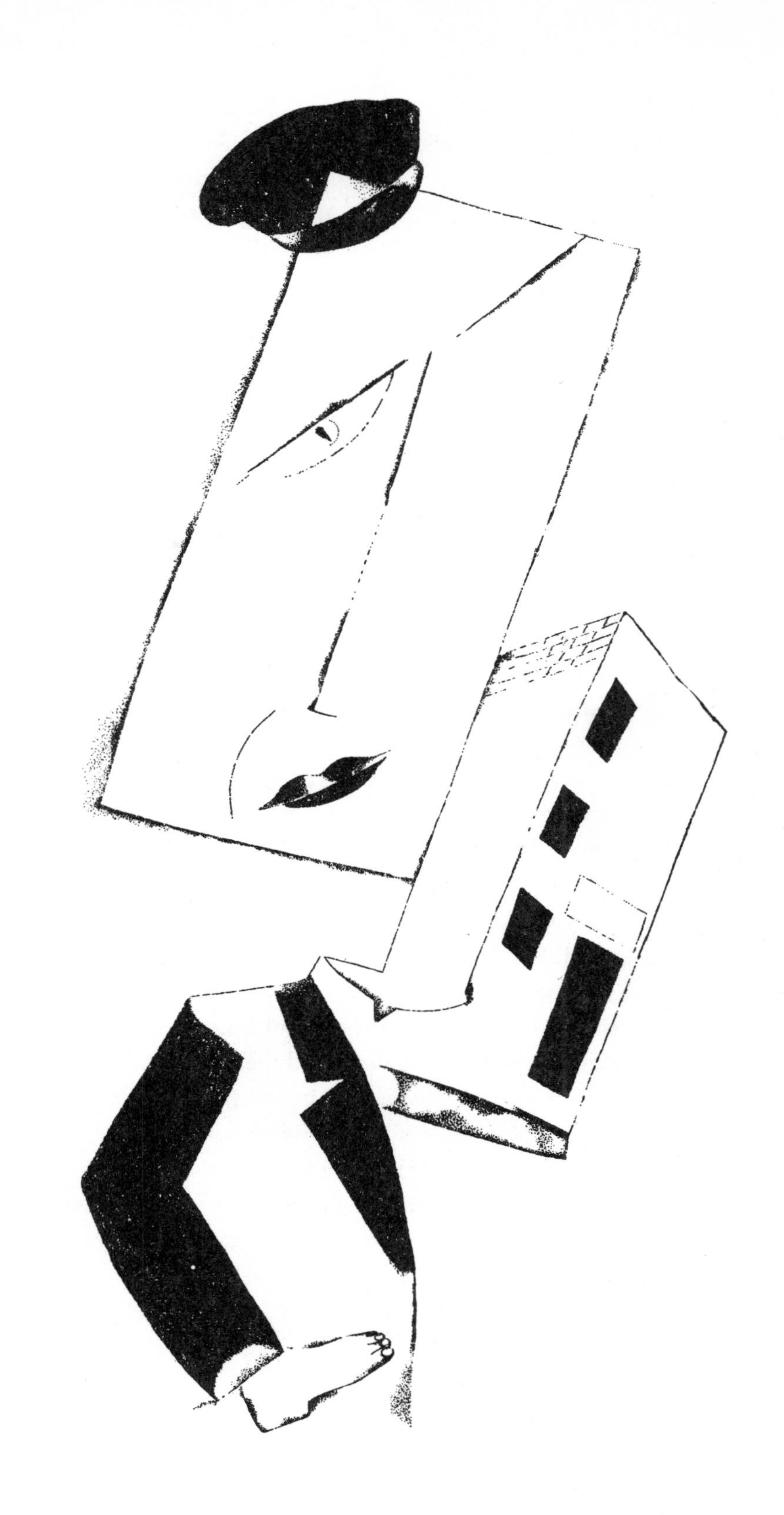

radiantly flooding light of the Ile de France, which lends a peculiar warmth and inspiration to natural phenomena and to men and their ideas and sensations? Or was it the power of tradition combined with the revolutionary progressiveness of the new artistic trends that created this unparalleled fascination?

The *élan vital* of this spirit not only drew towards it the most various individuals, peoples and races, but also derived fresh nutriment from them. Thus the untamed quality of the Spanish character, as incorporated in Picasso, and of the Russian, as embodied in Stravinsky, contributed a stimulating spice to the artistic life of this city. It lent French logic and its rational formative power that element of dramatic and lyrical vigour without which this second 'heroic epoch' of French art could not have ripened to maturity.

Cézanne had only been dead a few years. The monumental torso of his *Bathers* blazed forth like a manifesto that had to be put step by step into effect. The Fauves, the Wild Men, including Matisse, Derain and Rouault, who followed the Impressionists and the Neo-Impressionists, demanded that the forms and colours into which the picture was transposed should exercise a more intense effect than was usually expected of them. The painting should no longer arouse in the spectator the illusion of reality, but should awaken in him the same tensions that the painter had experienced in front of the phenomena depicted. The Cubists finally went a step further with their demand that the picture should no longer be a transposition of nature, but should itself *be* nature. The facetious expression *cubisme* became the watchword for an endeavour that spontaneously found its philosophical and artistic defenders.

The Cubists wanted to present phenomena in their eternal existence, free from the fetters that bound them to space and time. They sought to attain to the idea, the poetic content and core, to absolute beauty, to the 'picture in itself'. In their mind's eye they saw an analogy with music, which does not grip man by reminding him of the sounds of nature, nor by the beauty of individual notes, but always by the mutual tension of notes, rhythms and harmonies.

Cézanne had already described the effects of colour as *états d'âme*, *exaltations de sentiment*, and *vision*. One interpreter of Cubism believes that this style represents a victorious advance by the imaginative East and a weakening of the Graeco-Latin orderliness that had determined the structure of French painting for centuries. He compares Cubism with Gothic architecture, in which Western severity of form unites with Byzantine religious conviction and transcendentalism.

The twenty-year-old Marc set out for Paris with a friend of the same age. The journey took him four days. 'I came to Paris as though driven by destiny', he avowed later. 'Words that came from my heart flowed into my mouth. They almost suffocated me, I stammered. I came with thoughts and dreams such as one can only have when one is twenty.'

Things that had possessed the mysterious and magical attraction of the far-away when seen from Russia, were self-evident, confirmed by all the manifestations of the exuberant life around them, in the Paris of 1910. Here the deeds of art were not curiosities divorced from the rest of existence, but symbolizations of life itself.

Chagall's companion remained sceptical. 'What can we poor fellows do here?' he asked his friend. 'What is there left for us to accomplish? Everything has been said again and again. The best thing would be to take the next train back home.' But Chagall saw more than the names of the artists and their works; he looked at the whole phenomenon of Paris as an invigorating ocean in which he was driven by all his impulses to submerge himself. 'I stayed', he states, 'and most important of all I stayed myself.'

He rented a studio in the 'Impasse du Maine'. On the second day after his arrival Chagall visited the Salon des Indépendants, which now admitted the Cubists, as it had already admitted the Fauves. In this exhibition Derain was showing his mountain houses and villages painted in a range of dull earth colours and cubistically compressed. Picasso had painted a cycle of Cubist portraits — male and female figures split up into prisms, with musical instruments. Léger was exhibiting his tubular *Nudes in the Forest*, and Matisse surprised the spectator with his figure compositions painted in broad areas and daring simplifications of colour and form that would likewise have been impossible without Cubism.

The same exhibition contained the ecstatically glowing and swirling landscapes and views-from-the-window of the young Delaunay, a painter who did not become one of the great, but who possessed the gift of influencing young, questing painters and acquainting them with everything in the new painting that could be taught. This kindly painter became the mentor of such diverse natures as Paul Klee, August Macke and, last but not least, Chagall.

A little later, Chagall moved into the subsequently legendary block of studios *La Ruche*, a building in a garden of the Rue Dantzig, near the Vaugirard slaughterhouses constructed with the timber from demolished exhibition halls, that still stands today but is shortly to be demolished. It has two floors with twenty-four studios of beehive dimensions. The sculptors lived on the ground floor, the painters on the first. Chagall took a room next to the one occupied by Modigliani. In this way Chagall came into closer contact with a few representatives of what later came to be known as the 'Ecole de Paris', of which he was one day to be counted a member. Here, too, lived Soutine, another ecstatic Easterner, who painted pictures of 'slaver, fire and blood'. To this house the poets Apollinaire, Blaise Cendrars and Canudo were frequent visitors. They all took to the new arrival; this embodiment of a character from E. T. A. Hoffmann was in perfect accord with their poetic fancies.

Chagall at once started to paint. The pictures he had painted in Vitebsk had brought him to the limits of what he could express with the means he had so far acquired. He carried with him a still formless picture of his future creations, and he felt he needed new means with which to give them shape. He seized hungrily on the Cubist slogan that form and colour were sovereign, free media of representation, while the assertion that colour should be apprehended as *état d'âme* seemed as much in keeping with his nature as the demand that painting should not be an imitation of nature, but itself poeticized nature.

One picture of this period is Chagall's first *My Studio* (1910) painted in Paris. The colours are more fiery and turbulent than those in the paintings of the Vitebsk cycle. They seem to have been put on in a fever, the forms appear on the point of dissolution, – the outlines are melting away, and the objects are transmuted into chimerical signs. The picture is redolent of the impetuosity of the twenty-year-old who meets the shock Paris has inflicted on him by intensified creative ardour. A fragile, high-backed basket chair obstinately spreads its legs among the scanty furniture in the room, which might be the stage set for a psychological drama in the St Petersburg theatre. This chaotic scene is a starting and finishing point at one and the same time. It is conceivable that from this point of departure Chagall might have embarked on a similar path to that followed by his studio neighbour Soutine, with his sanguinary and tormenting visions.

But the succeeding picture already announced the line Chagall had taken. It is a work as big as a mural in which Chagall returns to the theme of *The Wedding* (1910).

The scene of the picture is once more the street. But this time it runs across the painting from side to side. The street, the houses in the background, and the sky are split up into colourful, rhythmically interrupted bands that increase the momentum of movement. The picture is composed of green, violet, yellow and red triangles and trapezoids in unmixed pigment. The colours of the figures walking in the procession contrast with the areas of pigment in the background according to the laws of complementary colours. Formally speaking they constitute with their curves and rounded shapes a counterpoint to the dramatically

tilted lines and areas. The people are the same as those in the first wedding picture, even the water-carrier is not missing. In addition there is a woman in a festal yellow dress. Every Chassidic Jewish wedding procession was led by a woman who danced to the singing of the whole company.
The figures no longer dominate the picture spatially; they are interwoven with the whole composition. At the same time their demeanour has gained emphasis. The picture's contours and shadows are a multiple gradation of phosphorescent violet, so that the black that appears in the openings of the doors and windows in the walls of the houses becomes an active colour. Two green and violet triangles shoot out of the lower edge of the picture with their sharp corners pointing at the bridal pair as the chief protagonists in the scene.

In accordance with Cubist principles, the picture lacks Cézanne's *point central* with which everything else in the composition is co-ordinated. Instead we find here the *simultané* demanded by Delaunay, the correlation of various contrasting elements of colour and design with all their correspondences and tensions, which exercise a mutual influence upon one another, so that a manifest to and fro movement springs up between them and projects a time element into the relationship between the areas of pigment, such as the Futurists had sought to achieve. In its mobility and melancholy the colouring recalls a Russian folksong with its alternating major and minor passages. Yet all earthly heaviness seems to have fallen away and 'matter' appears to have become transparent. The people have started to float; the houses, the doors, the shop sign and the sky seem to be following them. This painting proves how much of Cubism Chagall was willing to absorb. He acknowledged the sovereignty of form and colour; he strove for a logical construction, without which his pictured recollections of Vitebsk would have dissolved into nothingness.

Although this painting clearly strikes the observer as the beginning of a consistent line of artistic evolution, to Chagall it was merely one work among many others. In all probability he did not even regard it as an experiment. Cubism fascinated and repelled him at the same time. It gave him the freedom he had longed for, but it faced him with decisions which – in accordance with his nature – he did not solve by intellectual speculation, but by the activity of painting. He wanted to put down his experiences on canvas in the direct manner adopted by the poets. He rebelled against the idea that the subject matter of a painting should be 'as it were, killed, cut to pieces and its form and surface disguised, in order that it might be brought back to life in the picture'. He could not prevent a kind of ambivalence from springing up in his mind: '... On the one hand I admired the brilliant examples of a formal art; on the other my soul, in spite of everything, relapsed into a certain melancholy and thirsted after a way out.'
He asked his friends the poets for advice. They did not understand his scruples. 'What are you worrying about?' they asked him. 'The way you paint is perfectly right. It's just the same as what we are doing ourselves.' And Blaise Cendrars dedicated to the painter his hymn *Atelier Chagall.*

Blaise Cendrars *Atelier Chagall*

La Ruche
Stairways doors stairways
And his door opens like a newspaper
Covered with visiting cards
And then it closes again.
Disorder, this is the land of disorder
There are photographs of Léger, photographs of Tobeen that you really don't see
And behind your back
Behind your back
Frenetic works
Sketches designs frenetic works
And oil paintings . . .
'We guarantee the absolute purity of our Tomato ketchup'
Says a label
The window is an almanach
When the giant steamshovels of the lightning raucously unload the barges of the sky and empty the rumbling dumpcarts of thunder
The heavens fall
Pellmell
Cossacks the Christ a rotting sun
Roofs
Sleepwalkers a few goats
A werewolf
Petrus Borel
Insanity winter
A genius split like a peach
Lautréamont
Chagall
Poor child beside my wife
Morose enjoyment
His shoes are down at the heels
There's an old stewpan full of chocolate
You see the lamp double
And my drunkenness when I go to see him
Empty bottles
Bottles
Zina
(We talked of her)
Chagall
Chagall
Astride ladders of light

Translated by John Dos Passos

For a time the poets who were striving for freedom of form and expression followed the same path as the painters. They sought for their verses the new 'poetic subject-matter', that was not to be portrayed by the description of experienced phenomena and processes but by the intrinsic means of poetry, that is by words, rhythms and subtleties of sound. The poet, they said, forms his poetic subject-matter as the poets of a century ago constructed a sonnet. Only the poets of the past had their rules, while the moderns have first to find them. They learnt from Cubist painting how to borrow forms from their everyday environment and force them into the order of the work of art; they watched how these painters incorporated in their pictures wallpapers, scraps of newspaper and the labels on bottles. The fragment of everyday world was dematerialized and simultaneously gained enhanced poetic 'reality'. Encouraged by this example the poets, too, began to tack together scraps of speech, exclamations and newspaper headlines from the life around them. They discovered the tensions between verbal images taken from various domains of ideas, they sought an 'alchemy of words'.

Applying this new system of poetics, Max Jacob, Apollinaire and Cendrars produced poems that were intensely topical in theme and in the use of words and at the same time lent this contemporary subject matter the power of myth. The poets were soon to surpass the painters in the audacity of their vision. Although the Cubists tormented reality until it 'spurted its poetic venom', ultimately they were always caught up in the co-ordinating net of their self-created orders. 'Every poet has the right to say that a swallow soaring up to the sky is a dagger', cried Georges Braque. 'Should we not also have the right to paint a dagger instead of the swallow?' And Apollinaire wrote: 'Let nobody wonder if poets strive, with the only means they still have at their disposal, to prepare themselves for this new art that is far more comprehensive than the simple art of words. Here – conductors of an orchestra of unexampled range – they will have the whole world at their disposal: its sounds and phenomena, thought, human speech song, dance . . .'

The poets restored to Chagall faith in the correctness of his presentiments and impulses. He accepted the possibilities of Cubism as long as its methods of composition seemed calculated to augment his formal range. He was too freedom-loving by nature to allow himself to be forced into the Procrustean bed of rigid guiding principles. He avowed later that meeting Blaise Cendrars had been one of the crucial experiences of his life. He saw in this poet an ideal embodiment of the unity of art and life for which he longed.

II *Me and My Village, 1911*

In Chagall's painting of 1911 we find the same wealth of subjects and expression that distinguishes the Vitebsk pictures. They too are conceived in a wide variety of different manners. There is a *Bearded Man,* painted in large areas of strong colour, with big, sad eyes; green nudes that are magical improvisations; the first *Lovers on a Bench* shyly embracing. In the picture with the anti-Tzarist title *To Russia, Asses and Others,* inspired by Blaise Cendrars, we meet for the first time the Chagallian 'animal', the creature that is simultaneously cow, donkey and calf. It stands on the roof of a Vitebsk peasant's house suckling calves and human babies at the same time.

Over the synagogue roof that peeps up from the lower edge of the painting soars a maid with a bucket, her head is separated from her body. Chagall comments on this that he did not compose the parts of the body and the other elements in the painting according to anatomical or perspective correctness, but according to the tensions they contributed to the picture surface. He had no objection to the poet Apollinaire describing his earliest paintings as *surnaturel.* This headless, floating figure, or the body of a man sailing like a figurehead above the light of a street in *The Holy Coachman,* do indeed look 'super-real'. Equally fairylike is the painting *Dedicated to My Fiancée* showing a figure with a cow's head gazing thoughtfully into a vortex of limbs, parts of lamps, room walls and women's faces.

The first works painted in Paris were *études* in the various modes of expression and representation, which after a time condensed into more striking creations. One of these 'compressed' paintings was *Me and My Village.*

The drawing hand first broke the canvas up into circles with charcoal. The meeting and intersection of the arcs produced segments, acute — and obtuse-angled areas, that had to be brought to life with pigment – green, red, white and blue. From the capricious play of lines, colours, surfaces and areas developed a serious purpose. They grouped themselves according to the demands of pictorial logic; from the liberty of casual drawing grew the liberating order imposed by the development of the painting.

Chagall was too much possessed by his inner faces to remain content with the play of abstract correspondences. So the curves, lines and areas grew together into a green man's head, a peasant countenance with astonished lips and dreaming eyes mirroring the brightness of Russian winter nights.

The other side of the picture condensed into an animal's head shimmering in mystic white. The remaining areas he dissolved in pastel shades, at many points he caused the particles of colour to glow like the dust of ecliptic prominences, to sparkle like beads on a necklace or interlace in a cloud of drifting seeds that give birth to a flowering tree in the man's hand. Larger areas demanded to be animated with more definitely meaningful details: a cow and a milkmaid glimmer inside the animal's head; a reaper with a scythe and a woman head downwards pointing the way float along the pink street, that might also be a piece of sky. At the edge of this road stand a series of six buildings, two the right way up, two upside down, another two the right way up. Thus in the end Vitebsk rings out again, the advance into new artistic territory reveals the old and familiar clad in a magical brilliance.

Plastic Sense

The Frenchman's intelligence and logic radiate from even the most sensitive creations of his art. He has a feeling for the plastic values of a work of art.
When the Frenchman speaks of the plastic quality of colour, composition and pictorial space he means the colour, the interrelationship of forms and the spatial components as autonomous artistic means. These plastic elements are the media through which the visible, tangible, i.e. concrete, constituents of a picture are manifested. The work of art should not suggest the illusion of beautiful things; through its own means it should itself be an artistic object.
Cézanne found that the first patch of colour the painter puts on the canvas, and the first stroke of the design, begin to determine the values, extension and limits of the colours that follow. Each new element relates to its predecessors, the parts subordinate themselves to the whole. The painter cannot paint or draw arbitrarily; as it moves across the paper his hand is guided by the colours and shapes already there. Since all repetition diminishes the *frisson* of the incommunicable – and this is what the painter is forever trying to conjure up in his work – he must avoid repetition. This means that the painter's inventiveness, inner tension, sensibility and intelligence play an equal part in the creative processes involved in making a picture.

Painters have invented a very subtle grammar of their signs. The desire for change has become a passion with them. It makes a difference whether the painter lays on his colour in a glaze, dry, or impasto, whether he dabs it on or builds it up with a palette knife; whether he carefully traces a fine line or allows it to grow out of itself, whether the line is a series of hesitant touches or a self-confident sweep. The painter may allow chromatic tones to come into being fortuitously, or he may lay them on with intense intellectual concentration and animate them with sensibility.

The line has its truth, and paint may express itself as matter that has been made to sing. It is the corporate effect of all these plastic elements that gives a picture its own particular physiognomy. He is a good spectator of art who is capable of playing his part in bringing the actions and sensations in the picture to spiritual and sensual fulfilment. Experiencing a work of art becomes a creative act. The non-artistic picture bears the same relationship to a picture full of plastic values as a landscape observed through a cloudy window-pane bears to one seen in all its breathing, scented, trembling life through a wide open window. It is this freshness that can be felt and experienced with all the senses that constitutes the picture's mystery. This is the mystery Chagall meant when he praised a painting of Franz Marc's for the 'wind' he imagined he could feel blowing in it. But this plastic sense also finds expression in the spatial aspect of a picture. This spatial aspect is not necessarily to be understood as three-dimensional space manifested through perspective. Space in a modern picture is comparable to the sort of space that appears in dreams, a space without breadth or measurable depth, that represents nothing else than a synthesis of the things dreamed and ourselves. We are always the things of which we dream.

When we dream we enter into the object we have dreamed as into a fruit capsule in a painting by Bosch, become one with it, form a 'central coefficient', as the mathematicians say. We are always simultaneously the other, with which we enter into a relationship. 'The starry heaven of which we dream is the dreamer who covers it with stars', it says in Gaston Bachelard.

Just as the child sees space change with every turn of his head, with every posture of his body, so the painter too looks upon space as something living and mobile. Like the child he touches space as something material and is touched by it. These experiences permeate his consciousness and alter it, so that it finally becomes one with space. The drama of spatial relationships, surprises and contradictions becomes identical with the drama of our own sensations, desires and hopes, our joys and sorrows. There are spaces of delight and celestial gaiety in Fra Angelico, spaces of melancholy and solemn gloom in Rembrandt, and spaces of despair in Grünewald and Goya.

We cannot think the concept space without its counterpart, time. But these mythical antitheses, too, are only parts of a former unity that has been put to confusion. The unity is still disclosed in children's drawings, and the artist, like the child, lives outside the dictatorship of these 'two crippled Titans': in his work we glimpse the forgotten unity. That is why the irradiation of his pictures has such a liberating effect. It restores to us the feeling for the roots of our existence. Children and lovers most readily find access to Chagall's pictures as manifestation of *their* world.

In many of Chagall's paintings we meet the Eiffel Tower, that heroic witness to the Paris Exhibition of 1889 on the Champ de Mars. We need not rack our brains to grasp the meaning of this sign: it is a familiar symbol of Paris and France.

For the Cubists the Eiffel Tower was symbolic of the plastic sense and of art as a whole. In his book on Cubism Apollinaire wrote: 'The whole world is covered with useless monuments or with proportions that are more magnificent than the purpose they were intended to achieve.' A construction is not beautiful because it is a church, a pyramid or a bridge, but solely because it is beautiful. The greater its uselessness, the higher its utility to poetry. A piece of architecture represents nothing else than the perpetual conversation it carries on with its surroundings. More important than this, however, is its value as a plastic metaphor. Thus the mysterious dialogue the Eiffel Tower carries on with the clouds and the sky produces in the spectator a strange excitement. This feeling is expressed in a poem by Blaise Cendrars:

You are wholly
Tower,
Antique god,
Modern monster,
Solar spectrum,
Subject of my poems,
Tower of the world,
Tower in motion.

This hymn was dedicated to the painter Delaunay, who opened his studio window on to the Eiffel Tower, which he repeatedly celebrated in fresh compositions. 'The flash of its great rotations has not ceased to illuminate our sky', exulted this painter. 'The mathematical monotony of the circle is extinguished by the rhythm, the breadth of movement, the wealth of colour, the audacity of conception . . .'

It is certainly not necessary to put all this into words when we stand in front of the pictures painted by Chagall while he was living in the 'beehive'. But if we wish to grasp the complexity of their space and the meaning they had for Chagall and his friends, we shall do well to remember it. Whenever the Eiffel Tower appears in Chagall's works – even decades later – this symbol represents more than just a convenient theatrical property of a painter belonging to the 'Ecole de Paris'.

The certainty and artistic power Chagall had meanwhile acquired are shown in two further important works from this period. The first is the *Portrait of the Artist with Seven Fingers* (1912). The painter is sitting before the background of his studio. The head and figure are divided up in the Cubist manner; here again this method was adopted by Chagall solely as a means of expressing the visual significance of the forms and their plastic qualities.
The painter's eye is enlarged beyond its normal size, the greenish white pupil glimmers from the dark ground of the eyeball; it is turned towards the upper eyelid like that of a man in a trance. The curved line that forces its way from the wing of the nose into the low forehead in the shape of a fold continues the sweep of the brow and at the same time softens the severity of the square shadow on the cheek. The great pointed nose above the small, firm mouth and the spirals of the locks have primarily a formal significance; as in nature so in painting, a round form follows a straight one, hardness comes next to softness, the opaque to the transparent.
This figure, this face, do not enter into a dialogue with the spectator; they keep their distance from him, and yet the sum total of their parts adds up to an expression of shared emotional experience. The play of these prisms, trapezoids and segments of a circle with their rhythmic intersections and alternations, the living staccato of the lines and the complementary effect of the colours, engender in the spectator a similar restlessness and tension, so that the dialogue between the representation and the spectator as a partner, which appeared to have been prevented, takes place after all.
On the easel in this painted interior leans the picture *To Russia, Asses and Others.* Chagall lived with his creations as his most familiar environment. The painter's left hand points to the burlesque scenery of this particular picture, under the influence of which the number of its fingers has increased.
The curled and twisted hair might be flowers, the tie resembles a piece of mauve confectionery to which the confectioner has given the shape of a propeller. The scarf embellished with spots, the yellow waistcoat with gold buttons, the rose in the buttonhole – all these are typically Russian decoration and at the same time part of the formal heritage of Cubism. Is there any great difference between this exuberance of forms and the arabesques on the stucco fronts of Russian provincial theatres? In an account by a contemporary writer we can read the following: 'Everything looks as though it were modelled in clay, moulded playfully, with infinite delight in each individual shape. Giant fingers have formed the clay into rolls, cut it up into discs, and stuck these on strips of moulding. And

their colours are azure blue, ultramarine and cobalt, the walls are distempered pink, yellow and green.'

The palette in the painter's right hand, with its circling suns of pure pigment, its blue ponds and golden pyramids, is a perfect example of *peinture*. One must have stood in front of it oneself to understand the desire it arouses to run one's fingers over the enamel of these colours and feel their relief. Here the piece of canvas has been rendered precious with paint and a large part of 'abstract painting' anticipated. Chagall employed these notes of colour only in order to translate the picture-surface into a state of enchantment.

As though Chagall were not content with the Russian quality of the forms and colours, he also painted in a bit of Vitebsk, as we know it from earlier pictures. Clouds billow forth from the orange-coloured wall of the room, bearing the church and a few houses of the home town as though on a cushion. From the violet ground on the other side of the picture a window has been cut, the Eiffel Tower rises into the azure sky and a man caught in the prismatic beam of searchlights floats on the inverted triangle of his open umbrella. The street is darkened by the silhouette of a pair of lovers and the outline of a motor-car. Above the painter's curly head the name 'Paris' in Hebrew letters glimmers in festal carmine.

Amidst all the light-hearted gaiety that distinguishes these details, the figure of the painter remains powerful and masculine. This figure holds together the sum of compositional relationships and gives meaning to the individual details.

The scene with the Eiffel Tower, the flying man and the pyramid of light in the night sky crops up again in the second painting *Paris through the Window* (1913). Now the view through the window dominates the picture. The window-frame that cuts through it, the window seat with the human-faced cat and the Janus head of the painter in the right lower corner serve to give the picture a quality of strangeness. In respect of form and colour the Eiffel Tower and the brilliantly illuminated street constitute the central point of the picture. After looking at it for some time the emphasis shifts: apparently incidental details gain importance and the parts that initially seemed essential are reduced to the function of a framework. In the meantime the spectator has also discovered the elegantly dressed couple outside the window soaring along horizontally with the street and meeting head on; he notices the upside down train on the other side of the street and the locomotive puffing its smoke downwards. Finally he perceives the corner of the chair-back in front of the window-seat, which is smothered by the blossoms of a bouquet.

The cat with a human face crouching on the window-seat is the most mysterious figure in this pictorial rebus, a sphinx in conversation with the mask the man is wearing on the back of his head. What secret understanding links the masks, the animal's and the man's? What is the relationship between the toppling houses of the city and the pointed needle of the Eiffel Tower, between the flowers and the wheel-work of the railway? The painter's attitude to this painting is that of a spectator, as though he saw in it a stage that reflected his anxieties and home-sickness. In spite of the picture's jubilant colourfulness we can feel the grip of a strange power on our hearts, and we ask ourselves what Chagall was trying to say in this painting. Perhaps it is enough if we leave the riddle in the pictorial substance it has assumed, like the riddle in the fairy tale. Apollinaire was right when he called the world of Chagall's pictures *surnaturel*, and so were the Sur-realists when they hailed him later as a forerunner of their movement. Many painters who had come to Paris sought in their impatience to jump stages in their evolution. Seeking originality at any price they adopted the manner of those who had already 'arrived', in whose work they saw their own ideas and outlook embodied. In this way they became epigoni more rapidly than they suspected.

We have already seen that the agonizing discrepancy between volition and abil-ity did not exist for Chagall, that for him there was no gap between natural and acquired ability. In his artistic development there were neither detours nor blind alleys. Seen from the vantage point of the present, every one of his works stands immovably in the proper place in his *œuvre*. He himself reported later how quickly he felt at home and himself in the atmosphere of Paris, and how much he owed to the light, the spirit and the soul of this city:
'In Paris I did not seek instruction from academies or teachers. I found it in the city itself, wherever I went, in everything. It came from the dealers in the mar-kets, the waiters in the cafés, the concierges, the peasants, the workers. They were enveloped in that astonishing freely streaming light *(lumière-liberté)* that I have never found anywhere else, and this light flowed effortless into the paint-ings of the great French masters and was reborn in art. I could not help thinking that only this "freely streaming light", whose luminosity is stronger than any artificial source of light, makes possible such sparkling paintings, in which the innovations of painting technique seem just as natural as the speech, behaviour and work of the people in the streets.'
'I was about twenty at that time', continues Chagall, 'and was not clear why I had never seen anything of the kind in the other countries through which I had passed. Perhaps I did not see with the eyes of the understanding, but with the eyes of the soul. And this soul was furrowed deep by new and different influ-ences in the markets and streets of Paris. There I saw richer, more modern and more painterly still lifes than the still lifes of Snyders, and they were like those

of Chardin and Cézanne. I saw landscapes on the outskirts of Paris that were not dull museum landscapes like those of Hobbema or Ruysdael, but full of sensitivity, tremulous with the spirit of the age; and every chance passer-by was a vital enclosed whole – as in Cézanne, Renoir and the rest. Objects, nature, people illumined by that "freely streaming light" bathed, one might say, in a bath of colour. Never before had I seen such pictures. And it was the acme of a unique period of the art of our time in this one and only country in the world. From the streets, the squares and the fields one entered the Louvre, the French rooms, where the revolution in painting sought its origins and then left them behind.'

When we look at the works Chagall painted at this period we may jump to the conclusion that his feelings of happiness and the circumstances in which his pictures were born were in rare harmony. But the reality of Paris looked slightly different to the young painter Chagall. The Bohemian poverty of the studio in *La Ruche* has already been portrayed by Cendrars. Chagall's own descriptions confirm that his friend's view was no poetic exaggeration.

'When an insulted model sobbed in the Russian studios, when songs to the guitar echoed in the Italian studios, when the Jews carried on their heated discussions – I remained in my studio alone with my petrol lamp. The studio was covered with pictures and scraps of canvas, or more accurately with my tablecloths, sheets and torn-up nightshirts. Two or three hours before sunrise. The sky is blue. Dawn begins to break. Somewhere, not far away, they start cutting the throats of the cattle; the cows bellow, and I paint them.

'I am up like this every night. A whole week has just passed, and my studio has not been cleaned; picture frames, egg shells and empty two-sou jars of soup extract lie scattered all over the place. The lamp burns and I with it.

'It burns until its flame becomes hard in the blue of the morning . . . On the edges of my table reproductions of Cézanne and El Greco, the remains of a herring I cut in two – the head for today, the tail for tomorrow – and (thank God) a few crusts of bread lie side by side . . .

'No one buys my paintings, and I don't believe they ever will . . .'

During the days and nights of this self-imposed solitude Chagall worked on a large painting that discloses the more tragic tensions of his inner life – *Calvary* (1912).

Calvary

The most Jewish of painters and the most Christian of themes – how do these go together?
Chagall is no believer in the orthodox sense, he feels as little bound by Jewish as by Christian dogma. He is not concerned with the widely-held view that he is a Jewish artist *par excellence.*
Chagall has his own ideas about the figure of Christ and they have grown wider and deeper with the painter's development.
The painting *Calvary* passed through many perils. A German art dealer rescued it from destruction by the Nazis in 1933 and took the picture to New York, where it now hangs in the Museum of Modern Art. When it was first exhibited in Paris in 1949, Chagall said:
'The symbolic figure of Christ had always been very familiar to me, and I was determined to give form to it in the guise imagined by my young heart. I wanted to show Christ as an innocent child. Nowadays, of course, I see it differently. When I painted this picture in Paris I was trying to free myself psychologically from the ikon painter's outlook, as from Russian art altogether.' Of this Russian art Chagall said on another occasion that it was a religious, an orthodox art, and as such alien to him. To him Christ is a great poet, whose teaching has not been understood or followed by the modern world.
Calvary shows a division of the surface in the Cubist manner. Chagall distrusted the 'scientific' aspect of this conception of art, but he may have felt the urge to make these formal and painterly disciplines subservient to his new pictorial ideas, as though his power grew by this self-chosen resistance.

The ground of the painting is divided into circles and trapezoids. The largest of the circles changes into the sun, which seems to be undergoing an eclipse; its rays cut up the surface of the sky, which is laid on in fiery Prussian blue and green, and of the earth, which is Venetian red. The audacity of this colour scheme, out of which the figure of Christ shimmers in white and cobalt blue in the likeness of an over-sized child, underlines the extraordinary character of the incident. The cross is formed by the edges of areas of colour impinging upon one another. At the foot of this tree of rays stand Joseph and Mary. As models for this portrait of a father and mother Chagall used his own parents. His father wears a Russian peasant blouse and holds his bearded face upraised; the iris of the eye is turned inwards, so that the white of the eyeball shows. His gaze is not aimed at the crucifix; his upstretched hands and the expression on his face bespeak his agitation, the frantic distress of this hour.

Mary – Chagall's mother – once more appears shorter than her husband by a third of his height; her garment is costly and adorned with stars. As in many medieval Madonnas, one of her breasts is naked and she offers it in her hands to the child on the cross. The left side of her face is in shadow, the other eye is terrifyingly open. Picasso painted a face the same way in his famous early Cubist picture *Les Demoiselles d'Avignon*. For the Spanish destroyer of forms the resulting form was a new counter in his Protean game of metamorphoses: Chagall created with the aid of this simplification a Mater Dolorosa of 1912. Terror and Jewish *Angst* stare out of the eyes of both of them. Their hope is the child, who is bringing affliction to an end, who will perhaps be the Messiah.
The lower part of the picture surface is bounded by a river on which a man is rowing in a boat. Any symbolic interpretation that might be placed upon this river is irrelevant to the painting's pictorial qualities. These contours, colours and compositional elements 'happened to' Chagall as he worked on the picture. Chagall himself would shake his head if we asked him about the meaning of the river and say: 'I've no idea!'
A man on the bank is hurrying towards the cross carrying a long ladder. Who is it, Judas Iscariot, a scowling Russian peasant? Is he impelled by his bad conscience to take down from the cross that figure for whose death he is most responsible? Or does this Gogol figure appear in the picture solely as an ironically comic counterpoint, a piece of folklore, introduced into the fateful atmosphere of the composition as a reminder of the earthly origin of all things?

The earthly and the supernatural... For Chagall there is no distinction between them. His eyes, as he has always stressed, are fixed on the earth. The artist's task on the earth is his work, painting, with the aid of which he transforms what he sees on the earth into a work of art, into a piece of poetry; Chagall knows no mysticism, no symbolism apart from the natural artistic power of fashioned colours and forms.

Fervour for the Truth

The painter's endeavour to come to terms with the 'thing' as phenomenon, with its essential nature, its character and its formal function in a composition, reaches its purest realization in the still-life, the *nature morte*. It is significant that English and German on the one hand, and French on the other, have such different descriptions for the same type of painting.
The English or German painter is moved by the silent co-existence of the objects, their still life, while the French painter feels attracted by the chromatic

and spatial functions of a world of lifeless objects that gains life only in the work of art. In which of the two categories must we place Chagall's still lifes?
Chagall painted only a few *still lifes,* the Cubists' favourite subject. The earliest dates from 1912. It was painted in the heyday of Cubism; no doubt Chagall was stimulated by his friends' experiments. But a comparison between this picture and a *nature morte* painted by one of the Cubists shows very clearly the young Russian artist's totally different artistic purpose.
Picasso's still lifes were first exercises in a new way of seeing and painting that employed the knowledge evolved by Cézanne. The Spaniard was interested in the dynamic of forms, the weight of the tensions that filled the elements of the forms individually and in relation to one another. This gave rise to the manifold contrapuntal relationships that Picasso pursued with all his frenzy. He sought to wrest a magic from these forms by forgetting the familiar aspects of their appearance. In order to share in the magic of this new way of looking at things the looker – contrary to the manner in which the mystic sees things – must strive to deny the everyday ties that bind him to the object he is to remould. In so doing, like so many French artists, he follows Flaubert's advice that the artist should take up a position outside the world he is going to portray. Only thus will the artist be able to grasp the true function of phenomena. This procedure makes it possible to see the world, to 'free it from the dirty indifference' to which it has been reduced by habit and laziness in looking at it. The Cubists succeeded in their aim: we all know the refreshing breath we draw in front of a painting by Picasso, Braque or Juan Gris.
Chagall seeks to liberate the world of objects from their links with everyday life and tired reason in a different manner. In his still life of 1912 we meet once more the objects he found on the table of his studio in the 'Beehive' – the lamp, the bottle, the jug, the bowl of fruit, the cup with flowers painted on it, and the folded table-cloth.

At first glance the spectator might think, 'A Cubist picture!' Frontal and side views of objects are combined with views from above. The rotating shadowy cross formed by the folds of the tablecloth sets everything in motion, a new kind of spatial dynamism is born, gravity seems to have been done away with. Here too, of course, the forms are bearers of colours, and the picture, Chagall would tell us, must be comprehended as a painterly construction, as an indivisible unity of colour, form and composition. It does not occur to Chagall, however, to destroy forms in order to force their fragments together into new pictorial units; he is concerned, rather, to show us the wonders the everyday form holds for us if we will see them. Chagall looks upon the object he is painting as something that he is seeing and experiencing in terms of its own being. He does

not confront the world of phenomena as a critical observer but treats it as an object of artistic investigation.
In this connexion it may be appropriate to examine the Chassidic Jew's relationship to the phenomena of his environment. They become visible to him in the light that is identical with the grace of God. When God turns away darkness falls upon the world. In the imprisonment of the ghetto the Jews lost their sense of space; the light that illumined them radiated from a spiritual world. Their light was the candle lit on the Sabbath, and not the sun. Candles stood round the deathbed; they illumined the bride and bridegroom at a wedding. The candle whose light raised the nearby objects and beings out of the darkness bestowed upon these objects the radiance of divine grace.
If we give this wider meaning to the concept of a Chagall still life, we can say that there is something of the still life about most of this painter's pictures, even the rabbis, the lovers, the circus riders and animals . . .

Now, during the first Paris period, Chagall enlivened his remembered 'objects' from the Vitebsk landscape with solid realities. *The Soldier Drinks* (1912/13) is the name of one large painting with a huge samovar and a green soldier whose cap is flying away from his head. Another is *The Drunkard* (1912/13), painted in strong contrasting colours on a lemon-yellow ground. Here, too, the bowl with the black bird, the bottle, the fish and head, the suit and the knife in the man's hand are parts of a 'still life'. More important than this, however, is the way everything is in motion and seems to be floating and flying. This is not the movement the Futurists sought to introduce into their pictures, that were supposed to become a kind of cinematograph. Here movement means the denial of the force of gravity, of time and space in a mathematical sense, a return of the existence of objects to the realm of poetry, where everything is liable to metamorphosis.
In these last two paintings the Russian folksong, which never lacks an element of burlesque, has become an art-song, without losing any of its vigour. 'The new spirit does not seek to transform the ridiculous', wrote Apollinaire, 'it reserves for it a role that is not devoid of charm. Nor does it try to give noble significance to the horrifying. It allows it to be horrifying and does not belittle the noble. It is not a decorative art, nor is it impressionist. It is entirely a study of inner and outer nature, it is entirely fervour for truth.'

Four years Chagall had been painting in *La Ruche,* drawings and gouaches were piled up on the floor, canvases were stacked against the wall. Although he had submitted paintings to the Salon des Indépendants every year, and although a picture had once been accepted by the Salon d'Automne, he had never sold anything; when friends praised a picture he made a present of it. But in spring 1914 Cendrars managed to persuade the art dealer Malpel to enter into a contract with Chagall. Chagall was to paint seven pictures a month and receive 250 francs for them, that is to say, 35 francs a picture. Three pictures Chagall had sent to the Salon of the Independents at Amsterdam were bought by one purchaser for 900 francs, but Chagall never saw the money, because the Gallery's cashier absconded with it to America.

One evening Chagall, as he often did, went round to see Apollinaire, at whose lodgings a group of painters, poets and musicians were accustomed to foregather. A new guest was getting himself talked about, a German. Apollinaire introduced Chagall to the owlish-looking man: 'You know what you must do, Herr Walden? You must put on an exhibition of this young man's works. Do you know him? Chagall...'

Herwarth Walden was the founder of the German Expressionist movement *Der Sturm* and editor of a periodical of the same name. Kokoschka had painted and drawn him: a pale, nervously twitching face, above the sharply projecting nose arched a huge cranium. The short-sighted eyes looked out behind thick spectacle lenses, his hair fell down over his neck à la Franz Liszt...

Walden instinctively spotted the exceptional quality in the Russian's nature and work. This was a man he could do with. In three small back rooms in the Potsdamerstrasse, that were at once editorial office, studio and gallery, he had exhibited French Cubists, Italian Futurists and young Russians – the *Herde farbenkleckesender Brüllaffen,* the 'gang of paint-spattering howling-monkeys', as the Berlin press called them. More than 300 works of *avant-garde* European art had been exhibited in his *Herbstsalon 1913,* including some by Chagall. *Sturm* exhibitions had found their way as far afield as Japan and Canada.

Was not this Chagall the synthesis of Expressionism, Cubism and Futurism? Did not East and West, the Middle Ages and modern times, meet in the pictures of this black-haired Jew from Vitebsk who had chosen to become a Frenchman?

No protracted negotiations were needed at this evening gathering at Apollinaire's. The idea of a one-man show delighted him, and in the Berlin of 1914 the work of a brilliant painter of this particular type was likely to receive more attention than in the French capital of the art world. Chagall was prepared to

place the whole of his existing *œuvre* at Walden's disposal – more than two hundred oil paintings, drawings and gouaches, and most of them were and remained unframed.
So this noteworthy exhibition, of great importance for the evolution of modern German art, took place in April 1914. Chagall's canvases hung so close that they touched on the walls of the *Sturm* galleries, the tables and floors were covered with his drawings. The catalogue of the exhibition contained Apollinaire's poem *Rotsoge:*

To the painter Chagall

Your scarlet face your biplane convertible into hydroplane
Your round house where a smoked herring swims
I must have a key to eyelids
It's a good thing we have seen Mr Panado
And we are easy on that score
What do you want my old pal M.D.
90 or 324 a man in the air a calf who gazes out of the belly of its mother
I looked a long while along the roads
So many eyes are closed at the roadside
The wind sets the willow groves weeping
Open open open open open
Look but look now
The old man is bathing his feet in the basin
Una volta ho inteso say Ach du lieber Gott
And I began to cry reminiscing over our childhoods
And you show me a dreadful purple
This little painting where there is a cart which reminded me of the day
A day made out of pieces of mauves yellows blues greens and reds
When I left for the country with a charming chimney holding its bitch in leash
I had a reed pipe which I would not have traded for a French Marshal's baton
There aren't any more of them I haven't my little reed pipe any more
The chimney smokes far away from me Russian cigarettes
Its bitch barks against the lilacs
And the vigil lamp is burned out
On the dress petals have fallen
Two gold rings near some sandals
Kindle in the sun
While your hair is like the trolley cable
Across Europe arrayed in little many-coloured fires.

Translated by James Johnson Sweeney

In June Chagall himself went to Berlin. But more important than the exhibition was his wish to see Bella again. From Berlin it was not so far to Vitebsk. Moreover, it so happened that his youngest sister was getting married. The family were hoping he would come.
After four years of separation the name of an actor had cropped up every now and then between the protestations of love in Bella's last letters. This had reinforced Chagall's conviction that it was time to see his beloved and ask her to become his wife.
He stayed only a few days in Berlin. As he travelled on to Vitebsk dreaming of his imminent meeting with Bella, he little thought that the clouds of a world conflagration were gathering behind him.

Every Picture an Embrace

After the fascinating artistic life and liberating breadth of Paris, Vitebsk seemed to Chagall on his return like a toy village. His love for Bella and Bella's affection for him, however, created in him another kind of freedom and happiness whose reflection suddenly lent the phenomena of his birthplace a touch of greatness. In memory this town had already been more to him than an optically perceptible theme: it held his origin and his youth, his race and his faith. When he met his sweetheart again, Chagall relates, neither of them could refrain from tears. Chagall had been brought up in the belief that the adored being must remain an object of shy veneration. Now he could receive Bella's love in all its boundlessness and lavish his own upon her.
'What about the actor?' was his first question to her. A triumphant 'Nothing, nothing at all!' set the seal upon her present and her future love. There followed blissful days for Marc both as man and artist; there was no difference in the experiences he derived from the world, from love and from art.

His coming pictures shared in the feeling of newly won happiness; he began to paint immediately he returned home. Two critics who were amongst Chagall's friends at the time, Tugendhold and Efross, wrote about these Vitebsk paintings of Chagall. 'The influence of Paris', says the former, 'made its appearance precisely when Chagall entered anew into his home province, after his return. He painted the same subjects that had previously held him in their spell, but they already bore witness not only to a childlike poetic feeling, but to the masterly skill of the mature artist. The whole of Chagall's world, without any sacrifice of its mystic quality, had become more objectively tangible. Chagall learnt to see dreams while he was awake, in the midst of the sober day. But his return

III *Rabbi, 1912*

home also gave his vision a certain touch of tender feeling, it softened his satyrical angularity and strident brilliance of colour.'

'His return was like a healing balm', comments the second critic. 'He came back into his Jewish small-town world like the prodigal son into his father's house. He attached himself to this world with the same spiritual fire and force with which, in Paris, he had broken and crumbled its pitiful forms. The paintings of Chagall's Vitebsk cycle are imbued with a feverish, sobbing upsurge of emotion, and Chagall's capacity for work, which has always been great, was here boundless. Chagall painted dozens of pictures, and every one of them is like an embrace.'

What pictures were these that evoked the astonishment of his friends? There is a *Self-Portrait* (1914), one of the many that were to come. Its colours and forms are softer, more lyrical than the Paris paintings. It radiates carefree happiness. The colours are laid thinly on the ground of the canvas and glint like pastel. The house in the background seems freed from earthly weight; the head of a girl is looking out of the window.

The young painter is wearing a Sabbath jacket, a light, colourful waistcoat and an audaciously knotted cravat. Above the white of the shirt collar rises the head of a poet with girlishly curly hair, a smiling mouth, and eyes wide open in amazement.

Another picture shows a lad lying in the summer grass looking up dreamily into the blue sky. The background is formed by a small peasant's house that is also a byre, together with a tree, a horse and a pig. The mood of the *Country Concert* from Stravinsky's suite seems here to have been anticipated in paint.

A second self-portrait emphasizes the romantic attitude, which, however, as always with Chagall, is free from sentimentality. The areas of colour in this face are held in a network of outlines and connecting lines, like a stained glass window. Its colours and forms seem to gain their power not from themselves

but from a mysterious light somewhere behind them. The picture glows like a darkened ikon and yet it is modern in the generous simplification of its forms. It is the face of a singing angel full of youthful vigour. To keep it from excessive pathos it has been given – like Gothic figures of saints – a smile: the smile of uncomprehending astonishment.

The Birthday

The picture called *The Birthday*, which sprang from the same feeling of happiness, addresses us like a gay tune. We see the interior of Marc's studio. The window opens on to the village street of Vitebsk. At this time Chagall was in the habit of working by his window, as he did not like carrying his painting equipment out into the open with him. The festal day has left a still life behind it on the table-top that tilts towards the spectator. The beloved – in a violet dress with a broad white lace collar and holding a bouquet of brilliant coloured flowers in her hand – is flying through the room with wide open eyes. The bridegroom, his head twisted round towards his sweetheart and his eyelids closed, soars down to her. The lips of the two figures meet. Bella told the story of the birth of this painting as follows:
'I took my bright-coloured scarves and hung them on the walls, over the bed I spread a blanket I had brought with me; you went into the corner and began to sort out the canvases that were standing around; you quickly took one out and placed it on the easel. "Don't move, stay exactly where you are!" you told me. The flowers were still in my hand. I could hardly stand still. I should have liked to put them in water so that they shouldn't fade. But I soon forgot about them. You went to work on the canvas with such vigour that it shook under your brush strokes. You made me float along with the river of colours. Suddenly you raised me from the floor and you yourself pushed off with one foot, as though there were not enough space for you in the little room. You went up into the air, stretched out full length, and soared along the ceiling. Your head was tilted sideways and you turned my head likewise. You came close to me and whispered something in my ear. I listened to you as if you were singing a song for me in your deep soft voice. Even your eyes were singing. We soared together above the decorated room, sailing along; we came to the window and wanted to pass through it. From outside the bright-coloured clouds and a stripe of blue sky called us. The walls with the gay scarves began to reel, they made us drunken. We flew over meadows filled with flowers, over sleeping roofs, gardens and churches. "How do you like my picture?" You suddenly came down to the floor again, on to your feet; you looked at the canvas, then at me; you

stepped back from the easel and then towards it again. "Must I do anything else to it? I can leave it like that, don't you think? Tell me if there's any place that needs working on." You were talking to yourself, in anxious anticipation of what I should say. "Oh, it's very good, you flew off so beautifully. We'll call it *The Birthday!*" Your heart grew peaceful. "Will you come back tomorrow? I'll paint another picture, and we'll fly away together again..."'

Chagall himself says: 'I never finished a canvas or a drawing without first asking Bella: Yes or no?' Such was his faith in Bella, and it became greater, stronger and more mature year by year, growing with his growing success in celebrating his beloved in his art, which was increasingly asserting itself.

The groundlines of *The Birthday* were laid down in 1915. But Chagall added further touches in the following years: it did not acquire its brilliant, festal note until 1923, in Paris.

One is tempted to attribute these pictures, and the creative energy to which they bear witness, to Chagall's unique state of mind at this time; but he was also capable of dealing with harsher figures and subjects. This is attested by a cycle of quite a different sort – paintings of Jews, rabbis, village scenes and landscapes.

One of the most important pictures of this period is *The Praying Jew* or *The Rabbi of Vitebsk* (1914). The dimensions of the seated figure seem to burst out of the picture. Chagall's artistic strength and constructive intelligence are revealed in the distribution of the planes, the taut and vigorous field of tension of the lines. One need only cover the old man's face and hands to forget that this is the figure of a rabbi, and feel the contrapuntal correspondences of light and dark colours, of warm and cold tones, pulsing dynamically through one's consciousness.

The decorative element is not introduced merely to enliven the painting, nor is it simply an incidental offshoot of the subject: it becomes part of a cleverly devised system of tones, colours and forms. When we uncover the face and hands again we experience with redoubled force the abstract, 'plastic' functions of the picture's elements. This is not the 'Old Jew' theme which the local Russian painters of the period used to turn into a genre painting: Chagall's work proclaims the unbroken vigour of the Jewish spirit disclosed by the creative *élan* of genius.

The picture loses none of its power when we learn how Chagall came upon his 'motif': 'One day', he relates, 'an old man went past our window; he had grey hair, a piteous face, and a sack on his shoulder. Can he open his mouth to ask for alms, I wonder? And sure enough, he doesn't utter a word. He comes into the house and stands shyly by the door. He stands there silently for a long time. And if he isn't given anything, he goes out again as he came, and not a word is spoken. "Come in", I said to him. "Come here and sit down, rest awhile. It makes no difference to you, does it? I'll give you twenty kopecks, all you have to do is to put on my father's prayer-scarf and phylactery and sit down there, is that all right?"'

This was the outer incentive, an anecdote, no more. Many painters would have sought to emphasize this ancedotal, picturesque element. Chagall transformed the chance meeting into a lasting event. He was not on the look-out for a suitable model who could help him to realize a long-cherished plan. This wretched beggar offered himself, and Chagall turned him into a rabbi in whose eyes smoulder the undying hope and unquenchable sorrow of the Jewish people.

The Jew of Vitebsk ist the title of another painting dating from 1914. It is distinguished by a hitherto unknown verisimilitude in the treatment both of the subject and of the atmosphere. From a crossroads a narrowing path leads into the little town. The snow-covered surface of the foreground, which extends to the centre of the picture, is filled with the cold white and blue of the shadows and reflections that curve over it. Contrasted with the play of these spirals of pigment are the ponderous, Cubistically compacted forms of the houses, towers, roofs and walls. While the emptiness of the foreground makes us feel the frosty breath of the broad fields bordering the road, affliction, fear and menace cry out from the piled up, compressed architectural parts of the picture. This impression is intensified by the solitariness of the houses; not a trail of smoke rises from the chimneys, not a face is to be seen at the windows. The heavy, impenetrable sky is grey with snowflakes. Out from its immensity comes the bent figure of the Wandering Jew with sack and stick.

This painting grips us for two reasons. For one thing, we see how Chagall can portray the chill and magic of the uncanny. For another, we feel Chagall's striving after a new form of 'reality'. Hence it is difficult to understand how Chagall's critic friend Efross, to whom this work was known, could say: 'Chagall is not sufficiently masculine. Like a boy in puberty he has not yet lost the immature roundness and swelling of forms. He is incapable of shattering his brush on the canvas. Threatening and terrifying tones are not in his armoury.'

The young Chagall had no incentive to cling to this new note – besides, he scorned to imitate or repeat himself. But it is important that we have also heard this tone: it gives us a better understanding of the unburdened brightness of his subsequent paintings.

One of these joyful pictures, which bears a resemblance to the sketches of the Fauves, is the oil study *The Barber's Shop* with the grinning old man in the high basket chair, the tall tarnished mirror that distorts the shapes of the bottles and the hairdressing implements, the picture hanging askew, the patches of light on the setting for a Chekhov comedy. We can imagine how young Chagall revelled in this colourful spectacle as he waited to have his hair cut.

The portrait of his sister Liza with the mandolin, and a sketch that looks as though it had been put on with a palette knife, *The Woman Ironing*, are equally light and gay. Here play with pigment as a material becomes the main purpose. The subject is only a medium that lends form to the paint and life and reality to the picture. His friend Efross interpreted this period of his painting more accurately:

'Artistic and well-chosen brushwork; now as it were licking, now scratching; here bathing in the smooth surface of the strokes, there scattering over the flat areas of colour glorious "Chagallian" dots, spots and patterns that are gay and bright-brilliant red, green and yellow – that jump and wriggle like the dances of ostriches and Chinamen on the jocund wallpaper in our half-forgotten nurseries; the surface has received studied treatment, here rough, there smooth, in places the bare canvas shows, at many points the paint rises up in globular layers, the strength of the tones is subject to a regular rise and fall, measured and restrained, like the swelling and dying away of the notes under the fingers of a faultless pianist; a particular soft down like velvet or peach-bloom lies over everything and arouses in the spectator the wish to touch and stroke the picture, to feel its pithiness: this is Chagall's palette, which turns the coloured envelope of his paintings into a kind of geographical relief map over which one can with advantage rub one's fingers this way and that, as one gradually becomes aware of the inner laws that govern the unevennesses, the hills and valleys, on every inch of the surface.'

The aim and action of plastic values could not be more vividly expounded even today.

War and Revolution

Meanwhile war was raging. Shortly after his marriage Chagall was called up for military service. His brother-in-law managed to get him posted as a clerk to the war office at St Petersburg, where he had to examine muster-rolls. In this way he stayed near Bella and was even able to go on painting. But he suffered under the burden of office work. Poetry remained the only reality he was willing to recognize. Many of the pictures dating from this period show no sign of the outer circumstances under which they were painted. Some of them, however, exhale a breath of everyday life in war-time, especially the sheets of drawings, that rise to the level of accusation and prophetic vision.

During these days there were soldiers in the streets and squares; in his office work Chagall dealt with the names of conscripts, the wounded and the dead. The Russian soldiers of the first years of the war were no longer picture-book figures with fat moustaches who danced the polka, swung round buxom girls, and tucked in before a huge samovar. That was how Chagall had remembered them in Paris. This time they were soldiers in olive-green uniforms, their faces set in domineering, robot-like masks. One gouache, however, shows them as staggering figures in a world gone mad, wounded men holding one another up, a military greatcoat covering limbs swathed in bandages.

Even more uncompromising is a *Woodcut* in contrasting black and white. The illuminated portions of the soldier's head, the bandage round the dark; bearded face, the great hooked nose, the lips drawn back in agony and the horribly bared teeth, are chiselled out of the wood-block. The drawn up shoulder shows the shoulder-strap with the now meaningless regimental number; an over-sized Distinguished Service Cross dangles on the chest.

The same face appears on a second *Woodcut* showing soldiers with their wives – a disturbing picture of a night-time farewell, of contorted features that cry out the pain of young love, despair and approaching separation.

Only rarely has Chagall taken the present so directly into his pictorial imagery. Not until the Second World War, when he himself was fleeing from the hordes of a modern Genghis Khan, did he paint horror and imminent death accompanied by the angels of wrath and sorrow.

He also painted pictures of more restrained dramatic quality. Among these may be numbered a still life dating from 1916, which Chagall left behind in Russia and which is known only by a photograph. This is *The Mirror*, a memory of 'that great mirror which hung there lonely and cold and full of curious gleams'. This mirror framed by a fillet decorated with flowers in relief has caught the image of a candlestick, that seems to be glowing from within like an enchanted piece of crystal. The reflections form suns, whose lights circle in concentric rings over the darkness of the background and cause the top of a table to glimmer like a moonlit plain. At the far end of the table-top leans the figure of Bella with bowed head. Before this figure the huge reflected candlestick acquires surreal dimensions.

Chagall was not only able to paint pictures at this turbulent time, he even had an opportunity of exhibiting the works he had produced since his return from Paris. In 1915 the Moscow 'Art Salon' showed twenty-four pictures, and in 1916 there was another exhibition in which fifty of his new paintings hung alongside pictures by Puni and Malevitch. He also gained friends. In the house of an art collector he met people who supported the modern movements in art and discussed their problems.

In the days that followed, Chagall lived close to the places where the most important changes in the political, social and intellectual structure of Russia began – St Petersburg and Moscow. There he went through the end of the war, the revolution, and civil war. Later, on being asked what were the most important events in his life, he replied: 'My meeting with Blaise Cendrars, and the Russian Revolution.'

Chagall was never interested in politics, however; he saw no reason to join the Communist mass movements. Naturally, he was shaken by events in St Petersburg, and he felt the historic importance of these days. He saw people massing in the squares, he heard the songs and shouting, the speeches and slogans, the shots and the cries of the wounded. But he remained too much enclosed in his poetic world, in which there was no room for hate and conflict. As a Jew he was thankful that the Tzar and his government, which had promulgated such discriminatory laws against the Jews, were no longer in power, that the generals

had disappeared and there was no more war. Although he was the son of a worker he did not feel himself a class-conscious proletarian.
Hence he was greatly surprised to hear his name called out at an artists' meeting in the Mikhailovsky Theatre and to learn that he had been appointed Minister for the Fine Arts.
Chagall was known to the first Minister for Popular Enlightenment in the new cabinet formed by Lenin, Lunacharsky. As a contributor to a Russian social-democratic paper in Paris, the latter had paid him a visit in 1913 and asked him why he painted cows green and why people in his pictures stood on their heads. 'Your Marx knows everything', was the painter's answer, 'make him rise from his grave, he'll tell you.' It had not been a pleasant meeting.
Nevertheless, Chagall now went to see Lunacharsky in the Kremlin. If he was to accupy a leading position in the artistic life of the new Russia, Chagall gave him to understand, then he would rather go to Vitebsk. Therefore, contrary to the wish of Bella, who was sceptical about this 'appointment', he was made Commissar for the Fine Arts in the District of Vitebsk and Director of the Vitebsk Academy of Art.
Many years later Chagall painted a picture with the title *The Revolution* (1937). It was much larger than most of his works of that period, being 6 1/2 feet long and 6 feet high, and contained over a hundred figures. Chagall later destroyed the painting, but an oil study for it dating from 1938 is still in existence.
This picture has a Breughelesque atmosphere. The people are milling round in a snow-covered village square. They come with ladders, poles, lamps and musical instruments and are accompanied by the animals of the village. Red flags flutter in the background. The painter is visible twice: once in front of his easel with Bella, his wife and muse, at his side, and also perched on the snow-free roof of a house as on a bed of love surrounded by cupids and bouquets of flowers. The Jew who once flew over Vitebsk is leaving the house in the foreground, dazzled by the springlike uproar and the light of the sun that has descended on the earth with its circles of rays. A flute-playing genius is being swept along by the whirling wheel of the sun.
In the square stands a table; on the top of the table a young man is doing a daring hand-stand. The crowd is applauding him, they have never seen anything like it before: what was on top is suddenly down below: they are thrilled to see ordinary logic so palpably invalidated. Were not the Communist orators attempting the same thing every day with their dialectical acrobatics, their intellectual somersaults?
Beside the table an old man sits meditating, unaffected by the tumult of the moment. At his side a little book lies open. Here the verses of boundless sorrow and hope continue to be composed and prayed.

Did Chagall see the Revolution as it appears in this picture? We do not know what moved him when he painted it twenty years after this world-shaking event. But his life and work had already proved that he was a preserver and not a destroyer.

Even as Director of the Vitebsk Academy of Art the activities of a propaganda painter remained alien to him. On the Anniversary of the October Revolution he gathered the painters and decorators of Vitebsk in the Academy, and set them to paint cows and horses from his sketches, in typical Chagallian colours and shapes, on banners and banderols. The marching columns forgot to sing the *Internationale,* they laughed and clapped their approval of the green and blue

cows. Only the Commissars were angry: 'Why are your cows green and why do they stand on their heads? What have your horses got to do with Marx and Lenin?' Chagall had already given Lunacharsky the answer in Paris in 1913. He had not changed, Bella was to be proved right . . .

Work at the Academy absorbed a great deal of Chagall's time and energy, he was not born to be an organizer, a bureaucratic planner. But he believed in his star and he trusted his colleagues as he had trusted the master decorators of Vitebsk.

During this period he travelled frequently to Moscow and Petrograd, where he negotiated with Ministers to obtain money for paints and canvas, and even for food, so that the teachers and pupils should not starve. But the Soviets were not interested in 'art for art's sake'; they replied that it was more important to rebuild ruined houses and bridges than to paint pictures. In desperation Chagall turned to Maxim Gorki, who was then seriously ill. Chagall was horrified by the frightful pictures that disfigured the walls of Gorki's country house. The mortally sick writer promised to intervene on the school's behalf, but he could give no practical aid. Lunacharsky helped as far as lay in his power, but then difficulties arose from within the ranks of Chagall's own colleagues.

In his absence they intrigued against him and stirred up the students against their Principal. Malevitch was his bitterest opponent: he reproached Chagall with clinging to liberal ideas and declared that his art was not revolutionary enough. Only 'Suprematist' painting, which he, Malevitch, advocated – intellectually devised compositions of vertical and horizontal bars of colour on a monochrome ground – corresponded to the revolutionary artistic dialectic.

Chagall fled to Moscow. When the students called him back he returned once more, but only to discover that it was impossible for him to remain at the Academy.

Chagall later said of this period:

'I became Director of an Academy. I called to my school men of the trade, house-painters for example, who understood their painter's craft better than I did. We worked to order in communal studios. We tried to bring art to the people. Gradually the old professors returned to their posts, while the newer ones had to leave their pupils. Proletarian art gave me nothing, but it stirred the hearts of a few. They wanted to create something, they wanted to build, they talked, they shouted and yet accomplished nothing . . .'

There followed hard times in Moscow; housing was scarce, food was short, Bella could get no milk for little Ida. They moved from one furnished room to another, and with each change they encountered fresh difficulties. Bella tried to sell her jewellery in the market in order to buy the necessities of life with the proceeds. Once she was even arrested. Bella's father could no longer help them, his jeweller's shop and bank-balance had been confiscated by the state. There were friends, it is true, in whose rooms they met, drank cold weak tea and ate horse meat, but everything remained vague and provisional. Sad news had also come from Vitebsk: both Chagall's parents died within a short period of one another. He was not even allowed to attend their funeral.

In spite of adversity he worked. Even in the pictures of this epoch Vitebsk appeared. It was as though Chagall were trying to overcome outer affliction by fixing his eyes all the more incorruptibly on the reality of the little town's streets and houses. He painted the crooked, bright-coloured fronts with their windows, the shop signs, doors, cornices and chimneys, and the busy life that filled everything.

The colour in these paintings is drier, harsher. Every battered gutter, every brick is portrayed with a delight in the detailed observation of reality. At the same time these scenes show no trace of the naive pedantry of the Sunday painter nor of realistic depiction of the poor intended as documentary social criticism.

Even in these pictures the Cubist displacement and interlocking of planes and forms is evident. Every area has a life of its own, every scenic constellation its vanishing-point, every part is perceived individually – and yet in the end everything is organically united. This is how Dostoyevsky once described his meetings with houses: '... I am acquainted with the houses. When I go for a walk it is as though each one, as soon as it sees me, takes a few steps forward, looks at me from all its windows and says, as it were, "Good day, here I am! And how are you?"'

There are other pictures which, judging by their style, we should have more readily ascribed to the happy days in *La Ruche*. At this period Chagall painted a still life that turned into a *Paysage Cubiste*. Just as the dreamed reality of Vitebsk made its appearance in the Paris themes, so present Vitebsk, shamefacedly represented by a length of street with a walker and a house, becomes an ornament in the Cubist arrangement of light, pastel-coloured areas. It is a gay painting, and not only because a light-coloured diagonal strip bears the name 'Marc Chagall' written more than a dozen times in fine Latin and Cyrillic letters. Did Chagall, blinded by worry and humiliations during this epoch, give himself over to the familiar game of days gone by, was he able to make a clear division between poetry and reality? Or did he believe that the condition of external want would pass and that the revolutionary period tolerated an ecstatic, anti-bourgeois style, indeed, that it justified a dash of eccentricity? Did not similar paradoxes flash out in Mayakovsky's songs?

In the same spirit Chagall painted the two Double Portraits of himself and Bella, *Promenade* and *Self-Portrait with a Wineglass* (1917). In the former a young man (Marc) is standing by the river while his sweetheart (Bella) floats down towards him from the air like an angel. In the latter Marc is sitting astride his wife's shoulders holding aloft a glass of red wine while their daughter Ida soars above their heads in the guise of a baroque angel.

The colours of this second painting are as gay as the faces of the lovers: the young man's coat is red, the stockings of the woman in the low-fronted, slit-skirted snow-white ball dress are violet, and mother-of-pearl the fan in her hand. In the background we see the great bridge that links the river bank with the panorama of Vitebsk. The sky is a radiant blue, the water sparkles like an emerald.

Alongside these apotheoses of the delights of love, these colourful compositions of dancing surfaces in a major key, the same period saw the birth of pictures of a harsher character. Chagall had not forgotten his visit to his parents' grave. The encounter had affected him deeply and set up in him tensions such as he had never known before. The outcome was the series of paintings of *The Cemetery* (1917). In these he consciously harnesses the cubic treatment of planes and the dynamic interlocking of forms, spaces and edges to the aim of pictorial communication. There are late medieval woodcuts in which the graves open and the skeletons rise in a *danse macabre.*

Chagall only painted the tombstones, but he painted them with such forcefulness that we can feel the living presence of the ghosts that float invisibly around them. The earth is torn open, the stones and the burial chambers of the rich are in motion. Like a *mene tekel* the ghostly Hebrew letters drift across the picture. The wide gate has burst open and the sky is shattered as though by the tuba note of the Last Trump. One of the pictures is painted in brown ochre and pale pink; the other, with the gate and the tree hanging over it, in deep sea-green, blue and indigo black.

Once we have caught this new note in Chagall we plumb new and unexpected depths. 'L'odeur du monde a changé', wrote Duhamel. There are no spontaneous changes of style in Chagall's work, only increases in density which render the central point yet more manifest, and the mystery that radiates from it.

Entirely immersed in the masculine melancholy of this new vision is *The Green Violinist* (1917). This is no longer the anecdotal idyll of Chagall's violin-playing Uncle Neuch on the roof. It echoes from other dimensions of existence, the same from which Job in his agony drew the strength for his prophetic lamentations.

In addition to the expressive medium of pure painting, Chagall was also attracted by the possibilities of expression offered by a more comprehensive artistic framework – that of the theatre. In Paris Cocteau had voiced the demand that in the work of art of the future all the Muses should have a share. Chagall believed that he could realize a part of this vision in his own immediate environment. As early as 1911 Tugendhold had indicated that he considered Chagall capable of designing effective scenery for the 'psychological drama', which producers in Moscow and St Petersburg were striving after. He had encouraged Tairov to have Chagall design the décor for *The Merry Wives of Windsor*. It remained merely a suggestion. Not until 1917 did Chagall receive a commission to paint several curtains for a gala performance in honour of Gogol at the Hermitage Theatre, Petrograd.

Meanwhile the State Jewish Theatre had been formed and was directed by Granovsky, a Petrograd-born producer. In his autobiography Chagall writes:
'Round about 1919 a Yiddish experimental theatre came from Petrograd with an unknown director. He probably visited our town only because his wife came from Vitebsk. His ensemble consisted of a company of old and young actors. After the performance I was dawdling about in the foyer of the municipal theatre, in rather a bad mood, with my old teacher, Judah Pen, who always exasperated me with his cold, sceptical smile. No one knew what he was smiling about... Finally I stumbled upon the Producer himself.
'Alexy Granovsky, tall, blond and lithe, looked at me in a friendly manner. He rarely opened his mouth – perhaps because of his bad teeth. He could talk with closed eyes. Every now and then his eyes used to smile with a pleasure that suddenly came over him like the attack of a fly. And he always looked at one, and at the person by one's side, both at the same time. "You, Chagall, I need you", he exclaimed suddenly. "You know, I've got a play... just the right thing for you!"
'I thought to myself that it was about time I worked in a Yiddish Theatre...
'Shortly afterwards my friend Efross took me to Moscow to paint the walls for the New Jewish Theatre and design the décor for the first performance of the group of actors that had just been assembled.
'When I came to Moscow I found the chief producer, Granovsky, lying in bed. He was fond of coddling himself and playing the bedridden invalid when the mood took him. He conducted all his interviews from his bed. I showed him drawings I had made in Vitebsk... Granovsky passed a few brief and smiling

remarks that were immediately seized upon by the actors standing round as pearls of wit; they were supposed to run outside with them and, roaring with laughter, scatter them about the long corridors.
'I had no luck with producers. It was just the same with Vachtangov, who first had no feeling for my art nor the drawings for *The Dybbuk* I had made for the Habima Theatre in Moscow, and later instructed his own designers to paint in the Chagall manner – without me.
'I fared no better with Tairov, who had been bitten by the 'Constructivist' bug, nor with Studio Two of the Moscow Art Theatre, which was still drowning in psychological realism...
'All of them, and others too, first asked me to make drawings for their plays, and then took fright when they saw them.
'And now here was Granovsky. Certainly a man who was looking for something. But he spoke Russian in a Yiddish Theatre. He had talent – eclectic perhaps, but combined with charm. Only he was still wandering in the paths of his German teacher, Max Reinhardt, with his theories and mass scenes that were all the rage just then.
'Granovsky was trying to find something new – not with the warmth of a Jewish soul, but ponderously, as though from books. He was trying to get away from the German decorative method, and he was looking round for Jewish forms such as were already beginning to emerge here and there in the Jewish art world.
'I happened to be the first painter in the New Jewish Theatre. But Granovsky never spoke to me, he contented himself with a smile; and I, with my stubborn character, said nothing either.'

Chagall knew how he could place his painting at the service of the theatre, the Jewish theatre. There had been a Jewish theatre and Jewish actors in Russia for a long time. But they had often presented Jewishness under the picturesque, comic aspect, degrading the Jew to a type. Chagall had a higher conception of Jewishness, which he saw personified in the person of the young actor Michoels from Granovsky's company. Chagall's description of this actor sums up his views on Jewish art as a whole:
'What is Michoels's art?
'This is almost the same as asking what are the dreams and tasks of the new Jewish art.
'Goldfaden, Peretz, Sholem Aleichem (Yiddish writers) are to the actor what nature is to the plastic artist.
'The artist does not copy nature, but when he stands in front of it he creates it. In this sense artists and actors create a new sort of nature. And only this kind

of approach is of value to the dramatist and to nature; otherwise it is a mere copy; photographic illustration, not art. And one day, in a rare moment, the Jewish theatre succeeded in effecting an inspired synthesis with Jewish art; it began to live and showed the world its soul.

'As in the history of art, here too there were solitary great artists and a few less great ones; of higher value, however, were the artists who knew themselves to be in harmony with the whole period of art. There was the young actor Michoels, young and strong, although small in stature, thin but muscular, practical and yet gifted with visionary powers, with a logic that was mixed with feeling; his Yiddish speech rang as though it came out of our holy books...'

We can feel from these words how close Chagall felt to this actor. We can see how the world of art and the human ambiance determine one another in Chagall: now the reality that pressed in on Chagall was called The New Yiddish Theatre, its actors and its producer and the artistic aims, discoveries and experiences inspired by them.

This time Chagall was fortunate; he was commissioned to paint murals on the walls of the theatre, which consisted of the long drawing-room of a demolished luxury villa. This was in 1919.

The areas to be decorated comprised four bays between three tall windows, a long wall opposite and a frieze. For the spaces between the windows the theme was 'the ancestors of the four arts represented in the theatre'. Poetry was symbolized by a Torah scribe; acting by a cantor and dancer such as perform at Chassidic Jewish weddings. The model for this Old Testament 'royal entertainer' was Michoels. Music was represented by a Jewish street-violinist, and finally the dance by the buxom female who led wedding processions.

The long wall bore the *Introduction to the New Theatre*, a procession showing all the actors, dancers, musicians and acrobats, along with their producer. Chagall himself was not missing; he painted himself, palette in hand, carried to the spot by his friend Efross. Naturally, the Chagallian goat and the green cow also appeared. To the revered Michoels Chagall gave the mask of Hamlet.

Lastly, the frieze was an elongated and sumptuous still life with the utensils, foods and fruits of a Jewish wedding feast.

These murals are illustrative in character. On a ground broken up into bright-coloured bands or trapezoids – resembling that of the 1910 *Wedding* – the figures, the animals and the properties are drawn in playfully, the areas filled with gay harmonies of colour. The figures seem to dissolve the walls into movement and music. Here Chagall could play with the means at his disposal. Through his delight in the sensuous qualities of form and colour, which – as

IV *Gate to the Cemetery, 1917*

always – was coupled with constructive intelligence, he achieved a type of folklore translated into the artistic language of his age. Critics spoke, not without justice, of 'Hebrew jazz in paint'.

The drawings and watercolours for stage sets and costumes produced during these years also exhibit a strange integration of Chagall's formal and linear vocabulary into a Cubist-Constructivist framework. It looks almost as though Chagall were bending to the Constructivist tendencies of the modern Russian theatre of the day. On closer examination, however, it may be seen that Chagall breathes life even into the rigid geometry and formal puzzle of a Tatlin. For him the theatre, the stage and above all the play that takes place on it, were and are rhythm, colour, sound, movement, atmosphere. Chagall draws the following vivid picture of the conditions under which these works were born:
'Pieces of wood, cardboard, old newspapers, filthy rags and laths lay everywhere. There was always a great to and fro in the corridors, someone was taking a piece of black bread into his room, another a bottle of watery blue milk. A few people were chatting. And I stood on a ladder, busy with my murals. Ephraim the night-watchman, a wild young animal, brought me a portion of straw-bread and watery milk and stood there gaping at my painting. Sitting by the wall painting I felt the wish to paint myself, my village and towns on the wall. Bella came to lend me strength. She brought the little angel Idotshka with her, no bigger than a half-inch stick. She crawled about the floor and looked up at her father in the air. He was too high for her. Meanwhile 'Mama' went off for her Yiddish lesson with Michoels. I could hear her voice in the distance reciting, "Kleene Glöckele klingen..." And I sat there thinking about the new art in the new theatre, without the false beards that used to scare me like devils. I thought of the Purim players, of the beggar with his green face and his sack on his back, in which he carried his *Sidur*, his prayer-book, a piece of bread and a herring. And here I could see him at night in the moonlight with his beard, trembling like a tree in the park, and I wanted to paint him and take him with me on to the stage. In my heart I prayed softly to a deceased distant relative who once – what good fortune – painted a synagogue, prayed that he should help me...'
Another description gives us an idea of Chagall's delight at the effect his art excercised upon the whole theatre:
'For a long time I sat on the ladder in the hall, looking at the murals and the sketches I had prepared for the Sholem Aleichem play.
'I kept the doors shut. Granovsky rarely came in to chat about art, the theatre and the coming performance.
'One day Michoels entered with his short steps and said to me in a low but distinct voice: "Marc Zacharevitch, lend me the drawings you've got here, I'd

like to study them. It mustn't be like this – you here and we there, each one for himself..."

'And in fact I might have gone on sitting there for hours, finished my work, packed my bundle, and vanished.

'Michoels's open, comradely address was symbolic of the new type of Jewish man and artist at the beginning of the Revolution.

'I shall never forget how, a week later, I heard Michoels's voice in the distance shouting loudly to me: "Chagall, where are you? You know, I understand..." Then he rushed in, came up to my ladder, my drawings in his hand. "Now I've got it, look, Chagall..." And with his eyes full of joy, with a smile that covered him all the way down to his toes, he began to move, to posture, and to quote Sholem Aleichem's text.

'There could be no doubt about it, Michoels had discovered something: he had found the right intonation, the rhythm and expression, that is to say the form, the content, the new spirit, the new actor. It was a new world!'

The effect of Chagall's pictures was extraordinary. The people who poured into the theatre were dismayed, bewildered, amused, they stood in front of them and discussed them, and more and more people came. The theatre itself had become a side-issue. When anyone appeared on the stage to talk about the aims of the Jewish Theatre he was forced by the audience to explain the pictures on the walls. How far Chagall had shown himself a 'theatrical designer' was another matter. From a theatrical point of view his paintings were not an ideal solution: he looked at everything too much from the standpoint of his own pictorial ideas. His field of action was the flat surface and not the three-dimensional space of the picture-frame stage. There were unpleasant scenes when Chagall objected to the realistic properties with which the producer and actors spoiled the unity of his setting. A chair placed close to his murals was enough to reduce him to tears. The actors were to him no more than mimetically mobile parts of his painting; they ought to adjust their gestures and delivery to the rhythm and tones of the colours and forms. He would really have liked to paint the actors too – as he once decorated Michoels's face with tiny flowers, animals, a moon and stars.

It is not surprising that Granovsky found this self-willed painter an impossible collaborator. Chagall tried his luck with the director of another theatre, but again without success. This did not prevent these producers from subsequently having décors à la Chagall designed by other painters.

The *Narkompross,* the Ministry of Culture, appointed Chagall art teacher in one of the children's colonies of which so many were set up all over Russia after the War, the Revolution and the Civil War. This one was in Moscow. He enjoyed his contact with the children and it was at this period that he began to write down recollections of his life...

One day, however, a letter reached him from Berlin from the Jewish poet Rubiner. The latter enquired whether Chagall was still among the living, a rumour had got round that he had been killed in the war. In Berlin he was being celebrated as a great painter and his pictures had created a new art style – Expressionism. 'High prices are being paid for your pictures', the letter ended, 'but don't imagine you'll get the money Walden owes you; he is of the opinion that your fame is sufficient payment...'

Chagall had long ago realized that Russia had nothing more to offer him. Official policy in art was against him. 'The old masters of Impressionism and Expressionism have been liquidated', Lunacharsky had told a contributor to the Berlin periodical *Aktion*. 'They are incapable of doing anything and have not produced a single work of importance since the beginning of the Revolution. They are unable to do what we want. We need a classical art, full of ideas and movement...'

All the same, there were the most various groups of young artists in Moscow, among them one that called itself the Serapion Brothers and took up arms against dogmatic rigidity in art. 'Do what you did before', cried their spokesman Liev Lunz. 'Be revolutionary or counter-revolutionary writers, mystics or militant atheists, but don't be dull! Therefore look westward! Begin afresh!'

It was not so easy to leave Russia. But Chagall found friends who could help him and in the end Lunacharsky gave his assistance. Chagall was now able to cross Russia's frontiers with his wife and child – this time for ever. Berlin was the intermediate station.

Berlin 1922

In 1922 Berlin was the stronghold of German Expressionism. The Kronprinzpalais housed the work of its most outstanding representatives. The other European moderns were to be found in the Flechtheim, Nierendorf, Lutz or Tannhauser Galleries, and in the editorial offices of *Der Sturm* or *Aktion*. Even during the war, the works of 'enemy aliens' had been exhibited and sold. Diverse as were the artistic aims and conceptions of the individual painters and groups, they were all united by the word 'Expressionism'. Every group found its spokesman, who praised its members to the skies and reviled those in the other camp. Many first cried 'Crucify him!' and then 'Hosanna!' – like the enthusiastic Paul Westheim, who took up the cudgels in his *Kunstblatt* on behalf of all the

painters of importance whom a few years earlier, when Walden introduced them to Berlin in his *Autumn Salon 1913*, he had abused as a 'group of trained clowns and third-rate circus acts'.
Berlin's standing as a city of art was uncontested, even beyond the frontiers of Germany. '...The Paris of the past has largely died in the war, just as the Moscow of the past has died. A new point of contact is being sought. And this point of contact is Germany, the once despised and unpopular neighbour, which is daily being rediscovered by the Russian *émigrés*. Thus radiations of the Russian spirit from St Petersburg and Moscow, and in a backwash also from Paris, are converging ever more densely on German soil. Alexander Archipenko, who arrived from Paris scarcely two years ago, was one of the first to open the march from the west. He was followed by Kandinsky – from Moscow – long a spiritual citizen of Germany. And now Marc Chagall has been added, a prewar 'Parisian', to whom everything German is completely new and strange, but every one of whose early works is at present on German soil.' (F. V. Halle in the *Kunstblatt*, 1922)
Ludwig Rubiner, Chagall's friend, who had meanwhile died, had been right: Chagall had become famous in Berlin. Many of his works, picked up cheap during the war, were now in German private collections and galleries. Poets had seen to his literary fame. As long ago as 1916 Theodor Däubler had struck a blow for Chagall in his manifesto *Der neue Standpunkt (The New Standpoint)*, comparing him to the Tuscan primitives such as Il beato Angelico and Simone Martini. 'A cosmic child is among us', he wrote in the section of his book devoted to Chagall, 'the fairy-tale prince with absolute colour. Colour is heaven and earth. Where it blossoms everything is for the best; for fundamentally every strong feeling is good, by virtue of its sincerity alone...'
Däubler described the picture *The Drunkard* in these words: '..pure Struwelpeter romanticism. A blue youth is preening himself over a button on his jacket: he thinks it is the decoration of some Order. This he does with his right hand. In his left he holds a cigar. Though the position is ambiguous. What is it all about? An analysis of the soul of a child? Freud?'
The Dadaist Kurt Schwitters described the drawing for the same picture, which appeared in *Der Sturm,* in his poem *Anna Blume:*

Playing card drones fish, the head in the window.
The animal's head thirsts for the bottle.
On the hopping mouth.
Man without a head,
Hands wags sour knife.

The still life *Round the Table*, which had been acquired by the Hamburg collector Flemming, received the following interpretation:
'...In the colours rage the feverish passions of the blood, they flash lust, gleam madness, phosphoresce putrefaction and death. A titanic will intervenes, builds, fashions, welds limb to limb, so that the objects groan in the iron grip. An architectonic principle emerges, arranges, clarifies, safeguards and enforces the laws behind the mystic dusk of feeling, clarity of mind flashes as though pregnant with lightning...'
Finally, the lyric poet Willi Wolfradt celebrated the early Vitebsk painting *Death* in the style of his ecstatic hymns: '...A Golgotha sky sweeps along above the perpetual earth. The breath of death blows hugely at the sky, swells to a shrill pallor and hurls itself in a yellow glow above the earthly realm, so that living things stagger before its elemental force. The hurricane of the corpse's stillness lashes the conflagration of colours weary of life till they burn out with the groans of Laocoon.'
Literary as these attempts at interpretation sound, they, too, are among the radiations emitted by Chagall's work, the results of encounters in time. The biographer should also follow them up, for they form a new dimension within the painting's sphere of meaning, a dimension with which the picture remains in the future inseparably linked. It is useful to recall these interpretations when today, thirty years later, we stand before the same paintings; for the significance of a work of art grows with its history.
Whether justice was done to the painterly qualities of Chagall's pictures, to their value as a *morceau de peinture*, is another question. Tugendhold and Efross pointed out the painterly beauties of his pictures in their biography of Chagall, which also appeared in a German translation shortly after the war. Däubler, too, was acquainted with the concept of a painting's 'plastic quality' and appreciated it in Chagall. Karl With, to whom we owe the first independent biography of Chagall (in the *Junge Kunst* Library), recognized Chagall's towering artistic personality, but hesitated when he came to speak of him as a painter: 'Chagall's art is not characterized by a mastery of painterly construction, by a selective instinct for the form that has been reduced to its absolutely necessary dimensions, nor by structures that are curbed by a philosophical severity; in the last analysis he is not even hundred-per-cent painter...'
Naturally, there was no lack of disparaging voices. There were Jeremiahs who saw the 'carefully nurtured plant of a new German artistic volition' menaced by the example afforded by 'canvas-daubing enemy aliens': 'Where is the great creative personality, where are necessary, unitary, compelling and lasting qualities? We cannot find them! Russian folk-art filtered through the exacting taste of the boulevard. The mawkish portrait of his wife, a well-distilled, perfumed

art, supplied in flashy cut-glass bottles. It will, it must please a public that is either too uneducated or too over-educated to tolerate the harsh truths of an art that does not tickle the palate ...' (A. Kuhn in *Die Kunstchronik*, January 1923)
Chagall cared little for the literary conflicts aroused by his pictures. He was more concerned to locate the works he had left behind in the offices of *Der Sturm* in 1914. Most of them had meanwhile been sold by Walden, and the money the latter gave his erstwhile 'infant prodigy' had been depreciated by the low value of the German mark. Only after he had called in a lawyer did Chagall manage to recover at least three of his major works. It was a painful experience for him to be invited by Berlin collectors to see 'their' latest Chagall hanging on the wall. Nevertheless, he had the satisfaction of seeing the Lutz Gallery put on a representative exhibition of his most recent works.

Paul Cassirer, the Berlin publisher and art dealer, wanted to bring out a German edition of Chagall's autobiography, which he had finished in Moscow, illustrated by a series of etchings on the same theme. This commission was very welcome to Chagall. Unfortunately the text was never published, but the series of twenty etchings appeared as a folio under the title *Mein Leben.* The autobiography, *Ma Vie*, was first published in Paris in 1931, translated into French by Bella and with a Foreword by André Salmon. It also contained drawings, but not those in the Berlin folio.

Apart from the etchings, Chagall produced only a few watercolours and gouaches in Berlin. It is idle to speculate on what might have happened if Chagall had found a more sympathetic climate there. The conflict over the pictures prevented him from unfolding his artistic potentialities during these months, and it is not surprising that he did not feel at ease in Berlin, despite the sympathy he received from the painters and poets of Expressionist Germany. Many painters were affected by his pictures. Traces of his influence are visible in the works of Max Ernst, Campendonk, Georg Muche and many others now forgotten.

Today, however, Chagall recalls his stay in Berlin without bitterness; he remembers that he lodged first with a German diplomat and later in the Kantstrasse. During this period he came into contact with the painters Hofer, Grosz and Ludwig Meidner, and also with the actor Eugen Kloepfer. It is not easy nowadays to find people in Germany who met Chagall at that time. Only the painter and poet Ludwig Meidner – now over eighty years old – the famous portraitist of heads of Expressionist poets, can still recollect his acquaintance with Chagall in those days.

'... I had an opportunity of meeting him a few times. I remember a gathering Chagall arranged one afternoon in a studio in Wilmersdorf, to which he invited quite a number of ladies and gentlemen. Frau Bella read aloud part of his autobiography. The master stood meanwhile behind a curtain, following the reading with a tense face. I was sitting near him and was thus able to observe him for half an hour or more. Chagall had a very remarkable appearance, like a man with occult faculties, not at all intellectual, and not like a 'modern painter', nor like someone from a Chassidic milieu, more like someone who possessed much rarer qualities than any of these types. At the same time one had the impression that he was unable to act quite naturally and that he could not forget for an instant that he was the famous Marc Chagall. Later I talked to him – he spoke Yiddish – also about the East Jewish world, which was known and familiar to me. But he was not one of those artists who reveal their soul and spirit in conversation, but one of those who do so only in their art. He was neither 'interesting' nor witty, he uttered nothing that was unusual, eccentric or even 'fashionable', but showed himself a sensible man – although one could feel that he was inwardly burning with unrest.'

Etchings from Mein Leben

However much the line may strive to form the contours of 'reality' it always remains a sign, an abstract mark that receives form and life from the real shape it encloses. It is to an equal extent real and unreal.

Throughout all his creative periods Chagall has painted *and* drawn with equal fervour. There are the drawings and drafts for his pictures, which breathe the freshness of the first flash of inspiration. There are studies for many of his paintings, the earliest of which must be the sketch for *Candles in the Dark Street* dating from 1908, while other such preliminary studies include drawings for the portrait of Bella in the black gloves, for the violin-playing Uncle Neuch, for the stage décors and murals at the Moscow Jewish Theatre and for many later works. These drawings – like much of his subsequent graphic work – are often coloured.

Even a painter who works as intuitively as Chagall makes use of his studies and sketches, which he takes out again and again – even if only in memory. Thus the design of the *Green Violinist*, which was painted in 1917, goes back to a pencil drawing made in 1908, a lightly sketched study of Uncle Neuch listening meditatively to the strains of his violin.

Drawings have survived from Chagall's earliest creative period – sketches of his parents and relations, scenes from his parents' house and his first studio, landscapes and studies of the nude. These early drawings show a striking versatility. Many, like the drawing of the funeral procession preceded by a hearse (1908), are treated anecdotally, the elements essential to the theme being clearly drawn. Others, like the drawing of Uncle Neuch, are loose, almost impressionistic.

Then there are drawings with a reed pen, which yields to a liquid and flowing line. In others the drawing hand conjures up outlines that resemble ornaments. Here we meet for the first time the line composed of dots that Chagall later introduced into his painting. A brush drawing of a seated-woman with her head and arm resting on the back of the chair might be the work of Matisse; a study of a man with a stiff hat, dedicated to Apollinaire, could have been drawn by Modigliani. In the quality of line and general character some pen drawings show a resemblance to the early Kubin or Klee. Others again exhibit the elegance we find in Dufy or Segonzac – an interior, for example, with a lad playing the mandolin and a girl on a *chaise-longue* dreamily listening. A pencil drawing showing the sheds of the herring depot, his father rolling a heavy barrel along the ground and a pompous-looking merchant, gives a foretaste of his later illustrations to Gogol.
Was Chagall a good imitator, a skilled technician who could handle the naive dash as well as the sinuous line of the virtuoso? We find the answer to this question as soon as we immerse ourselves in the world of his drawings. We are instantly struck by their unmistakable and unrepeatable Chagallian character. The dots and two dashes placed in the oval of a face, a zigzag line representing the beard sketched in around it, and we are already gripped by the simple credulity of a peasant countenance. What a power of suggestion emanates from the drawing of the grandfather resting one toil-worn hand on the table while the fingers of the other hold the teapot, as he smiles shyly at the spectator. This drawing testifies to the honest conviction of the sentence that concludes *Ma Vie:* 'I am certain Rembrandt loves me.'
And then the self-portraits arouse our astonishment. There is the pencil drawing with the mysterious chiaroscuro and the wry yet smiling mouth dated 1922, which a critic described at the time as 'Leonardesque'. Then there is the drawing from 1911, in which the painter stands with raised palette in front of the onion-shaped domes and fences of Vitebsk gazing up into the night sky. We shall henceforth find this expression of amazement in Chagall's work throughout the whole of his creative life; its most recent appearance is in the triumphant work of his old age, a painting called *The Roofs* and dated 1955, in which the same youth no longer looks questingly upwards but bends down in grateful greeting over the red roofs of Vitebsk, still as a self-portrait, still a youth, and yet already a symbol of unceasing gratitude for a rich, full life.
If we wished to classify the drawings that precede the first folio, *Mein Leben*, we should have to describe them as the exact opposite of academic; even the 'studies', the life drawings and landscapes, retain the intimate quality of personal encounters. The academic draughtsman thinks in terms of systems, building up his drawing with the aid of calculated spaces and co-ordinating lines; he stands

in front of the object critically, measuring it up and reducing it to the level of a model.

How differently Chagall sees and draws. Like a child under the pressure of emotion, he thinks from one line to the next as from one event to another. But a line is simultaneously the contour of a form that gains expression, character and soul from the mysterious sources of its being. The tensions of living movement and demeanour in visible objects and beings, which are recalled to memory during the process of drawing, are immediately transformed into tensions of a plastic, artistic nature. Thus Chagall – contrary to Picasso or Matisse – does not proceed from form to subject matter, but from the dreamlike spontaneity of the initial sketching-in to a final result in which living form becomes gravid with poetic symbolism.

This creative logic born of intuition is evident even in those works which, at first glance, appear mannered – such as the drawings containing certain Cubist elements. But here, too, we can feel the quality of naivety when Chagall carries the taut line drawing *ad absurdum*, as in the Indian-ink sketch of the man through whose face a row of houses shoots, or in the drawing *Chagall* (1918), in which the left arm has become a leg and the toes, together with the fingers of the right hand, pile the letters CHAGALL one on top of the other like toy bricks.

With reference to this method of composition Chagall speaks of a 'psychic formalism'. 'If, in a picture, I have cut off a cow's head and put it on upside down, or occassionally even painted the whole picture topsy turvy, I have not done so in order to make literature. I want to introduce into my picture a psychic shock, which always operates through pictorial factors, in other words to introduce a fourth dimension. Therefore let people cease talking about fairy tales, of the fantastic, of Chagall the flying painter, when they speak of me. I am a painter who is unconsciously conscious.'

The first prints Chagall made in Vitebsk were woodcuts and lithographs. In style they were gloomy and sombre, even when Chagall enlivened them with colours, a practice which he never abandoned.

The etchings for *Mein Leben* are drypoints. This technique permitted Chagall to draw directly with the sharp steel needle on the polished copper plate. The line produced by this method possesses greater sharpness than the line bitten with acid, though this sharpness is softened by the burr that forms on the edge and holds ink when the printing is carried out. Shading executed with the drypoint has an attractive velvety depth, blackness and wealth of contrasts.

The themes of these works are drawn from the circle of his earlier motifs: the Vitebsk of his youth with the figures that surrounded and lived with him in those days. There are the wretched houses in Pokrovskaya Street, his two grandfathers sitting side by side gesticulating, his mother's grave. Many of the twenty works in this folio are eccentrically humorous, like the picture of the motorist, a dancing, prancing figure carrying a 1910-model motorcar on his head. These engravings are distinguished by the brilliant versatility with which the artist handles the graphic media, the fresh and positive character of the strokes and the bold distribution of black and white areas.
It was a curious coincidence that just as he was working on these etchings Chagall received a request for other illustrations – from Ambroise Vollard in Paris. Vollard, the Impressionists' art dealer, the writer and publisher, of whom so many portraits were painted, had already taken up the cudgels on behalf of Cézanne and Renoir, and later published a series of splendidly produced collectors' pieces illustrated by the most celebrated of the modern artists. The way in which he stumbled on Chagall, who had meanwhile been forgotten in Paris, is a story on its own.

When Chagall went away from his studio in La Ruche in 1914 he left behind all the pictures that did not go into the *Sturm* exhibition. The art dealer Malpel, with whom Chagall had entered into a contract shortly before setting out, felt entitled on the outbreak of war – when there could be no possibility of Chagall's early return – to open the studio door that was only fastened with a piece of wire and take possession of a number of pictures. Others learnt from his example and various painter neighbours took the rest, which soon appeared on the Paris art market. The art critic Coquiot bought several paintings in ignorance of where they came from, and showed them to Vollard, who immediately conceived the wish to have Chagall illustrate one of his forthcoming *de luxe* editions. This was how Vollard came to write to Chagall in Berlin the letter that had such an important effect on his development.

The invitation suited Chagall very well, and he returned to Paris in spring 1923, after nine years absence. He found his studio looted. For the first two years he lived in a studio in the Avenue Orléans – in the same house in which Lenin had lain hidden before his return to Russia. Later Chagall moved with his little family to a house of his own in Boulogne-sur-Seine.

Artistic life in Paris was no less fascinating now than in 1910. The innovators of yesterday had become the acknowledged masters of the Ecole de Paris. The erstwhile Cubist Picasso was painting his 'classicist' pictures that recalled Ingres in their form and Corot in their colour; Matisse was striving after a harmony of bold pictorial form with carefully chosen colours that worthily continued the tradition of French *peinture*. Having smashed the formal world of past centuries, the painters were doing their best to construct with the fragments a foundation upon which they could rebuild.

But the early post-war years had their *enfants terribles*, the Surrealists. They demanded psychic shock in art, their domain was that of the dream, the fairy tale, the gruesomely grotesque. They had learnt from the German Romantics, the English Pre-Raphaelites, the Marquis de Sade, Lautréamont and Sigmund Freud. Chagall, with his world of fantastic and ambiguous images, was bound to be welcome to the Surrealists. In his famous manifesto the spokesman of the Surrealists, André Breton, had already alluded to Chagall as a forerunner of this movement. But it was not Chagall's way to join schools or form groups of disciples:

'On my return to Paris I was pleasantly surprised to find a new artistic youth, which, in a certain respect, was rehabilitating the pre-war term "literature". What had been an insult in 1910 was now almost a requirement. It is, therefore, all the more regrettable that the art of this epoch has done little to distinguish itself by the natural technical skill that was so characteristic of the masters of the heroic age... Everything in art must come from the movement of our blood, from the whole of our being, including that part which is unconscious.'

Chagall's artistic outlook had grown firmer during his absence from Paris. He had experienced war and revolution, and for the first time he had been uprooted from his home and suffered artistic defamation. 'War', he remarked, 'seemed to me not only a school of life, but also a school of art. Far from the exhibition salons, the galleries and cafés of Paris I asked myself: Does not this war mark the point at which we must begin a reappraisal? The final forms of the so-called realistic school, including Impressionism and Cubism, appeared to me powerless. Trends which many people, through mental laziness, had scornfully dismissed as "literature" were now forcing their way to the surface. The war, it seemed to me, and the conditions of life that would follow it, would relieve painters of the need to create that attitute of "supplementing" nature which it was almost impossible for them to evolve by realistic, technical means. In future, life itself would enter the game and create additional psychic elements which art had hitherto lacked, and "contrasts" without which art is unimaginable and incomplete...'

An Honest Craftsman of God

In agreement with Ambroise Vollard Chagall had decided to illustrate Gogol's *Dead Souls,* that epic of human pettiness and futility whose heroes and actors – small landowners, officials and serfs – are nothing but knaves, cut-throats and artful dodgers.

In this book we breathe the fug of government offices, the vapours of crowded salons, we hear the provincial hubbub of their occupants whom Gogol the romantic, in his love for a finer and more upright Russia, drew with unvarnished realism. But in spite of the clarity with which he depicts his characters' human weaknesses, the author does not degenerate into a cynical caricaturist, but remains a philanthropist prompted by high ideals, so that the reader has to chuckle at these recondite manifestations of human infamy.

Gogol's novel had already been illustrated several times; the figure of the cowardly yet self-confident Chichikov, the daydreaming and sentimental Manilov, the arch-rogue Nozdrev and the miserable Plushkin had stimulated Russian draughtsmen to produce illustrations ever since the book's appearance in 1842, although Gogol – himself a draughtsman of considerable skill – would have nothing to do with any scheme for illustrating it. 'I am an enemy of all wood-engravings and similar modern fiddle-faddle', he once remarked. 'The goods should be sold as they are and there is no point in dressing them up in this sort of sugar-coating. Extravagances of this nature would only be permissible if they were really artistic. But where is a genius to be found for such a task...?' Hence the woodcuts made by his contemporary Agin, who achieved in these illustrations something almost on a par with the novel itself, were only allowed to appear as a folio without the text.

Chagall was more than an 'honest servant of the word'. In his own way he was also a romantic, he was gifted with acute sensibilities and a powerful mind, and he had given many proofs of his ability to portray the phenomena of his environment and yet prevent them from degenerating into flat reflections. While literary historians in the Bolshevist Russia he had just left were busy stressing the element of social criticism and the reformist tendencies in Gogol's work, Chagall put into his etchings the universal 'heroes' of a *comédie humaine,* who always and everywhere resemble one another, and he took a Rabelaisian delight in depicting them.

S. von Radecky's comments on Agin's illustrations apply equally well to Chagall's: '...His task was to provide the novel with support, to intensify the impression created by the succession of events in time by means of a fixed image that summed them up. He chose for illustration only such passages in the text as opened up, though only to the initiated, immense perspectives; here he functioned as a brilliant interpreter, illuminating the mental landscape with many flashes of insight.'

The following passage, for example, was illustrated by both artists: '...Pavel Ivanovitch's appearance at the ball aroused unusual excitement. Good God, there you are, Pavel Ivanovitch! There's our Pavel Ivanovitch. Let me embrace you, Pavel Ivanovitch! Give him to me, I want to smother him with kisses, my most precious Pavel Ivanovitch...!'

In Agin's woodcut we see a circle of men in evening dress and uniforms crowding eagerly round a man – Pavel Ivanovitch – of whom, however, we can discern nothing but a hand holding a top hat. The rest of him is hidden by flapping coattails and trouser legs. The scene is watched by some dressed up figures in the foreground. Despite all the charm of the drawing, this illustration would be incomprehensible to anyone unfamiliar with the text.

Chagall, on the other hand, makes of his hero's inflated head and the puffed out chest of his dinner jacket a magnificent portrait of the drawing-room lion as a type, a profile conjured up with a few strokes and occupying half the picture.

The other side is filled by the schematic and drastically foreshortened representation of an applauding audience; a lightly sketched in orchestra in a musician's gallery strikes up a welcoming flourish. The physiognomy of Chagall's hero,

though on another person, had already appeared in Agin's woodcut. Chagall had, therefore, drawn inspiration from the old illustrations.
Agin depicts a government office with all the scrupulous exactitude of a chronicler, showing every detail of the furniture, equipment and objects listed in an invisible inventory, together with the pallid-looking clerks. Agin drew everything in the same manner, whether it was a government office, a ballroom or a pigsty.
Chagall finds a new mode of presentation for every subject. In his illustrations the same government office becomes a sum of curly signs that look like numbers. Desk-tops, ink-wells, writing hands and long noses are dotted about in isolation within a circle, each item individually significant. A clerk's head grows up through the top of his desk, so firmly is he attached to his place of work. The doorway resembles a gallows under whose beam the office superintendent lours with Napoleonic mien. In this way Chagall translates Gogol's jest into graphic symbolism, transforms the word into a spontaneously effective arabesque, transmutes the atmosphere, with the tangible substance of its odours and its milieu, into a patchy, scratchy or soft and dusky black. These etchings are a meeting-place for the tragi-comic characters of world literature. From one page to the next we meet Falstaff, Don Quixote and Sancho Panza, Tartuffe and Molière's miser. As we recognize them we see in them our own world, laugh about it, and really cease to need Gogol's text . . .

Chagall's friend Ivan Goll has given an amusing description of the artist at work on these etchings:
'... You can come to him whenever you like – Marc sits there like a cobbler hammering away at his copperplates, an upright craftsman of God. His wife, who ministers to his art as a nurse ministers to a sick man's fever, reads the chapter aloud to him. They keep on laughing. Ida, their seven-year-old daughter, jumps down from the piano and wants to hear the story as well, and now the fantastic situations are re-created to the accompaniment of laughter by a strange family, with all the humour and tragedy of Russia. And father Marc, the craziest child of the three, makes faces, sticks out his tongue at his daughter, digs his wife in the ribs, pulls his hair down over his forehead – and draws at the same time ... For every picture a different technique, a different philosophy, a different outlook – every picture different, like every person and every day, how does he do it? One gay, another clear as snow, another seen through the magical haze of alcohol, calves in the sky and flowers in the stomachs of virgins; but what devotion – a Jewish St Francis of Assisi ... And all the time Marc laughs, makes faces, lets himself be pinched by Ida, bites, and groans his daily 'Je suis si malheureux! Je veux mourir!'

The Discovery of Colour

Work on the illustrations for *Dead Souls* was to occupy Chagall for a good many years. The finished etchings could not be published until 1948 – long after Vollard's death. But Chagall had not come to Paris merely to work in black and white: he immediately began to paint. As with many great artists, it is idle to enquire whether he painted his pictures while resting between graphic cycles, or whether he produced his voluminous graphic *œuvre* in the intervals of painting. Chagall, who developed his individual pictures after detailed preliminary sketches, also planned his themes and cycles well in advance. He frequently worked over old paintings, and the dates given for many of his pictures show that he spent years, or even decades, painting them. Thus in 1923 he completed several pictures he had begun years before in Vitebsk; among them was *The Birthday* which seems only to have been waiting to receive its final brilliance in the atmosphere of Paris.
Did Chagall's renewed encounter with Paris pass off entirely without friction, was his voice strong enough immediately to make itself heard in the chorus of other voices? As early as 1924 the Galerie Barbazanges put on a retrospective exhibition that made artistic Paris, which seemed to have forgotten Chagall, sit up and take notice.

v *The Girl Acrobat, 1930*

'Chagall, a God for Russia, a genius for Germany, was almost spat upon, and greeted by some journalists as an undesirable guest and alien', wrote Yvan Goll. 'It takes ten years of intense and stubborn struggle to gain a leading position in the art world of Paris. But Chagall is like a child or a woman: inexperienced in life, he nevertheless possesses, like the illuminati, unerring psychological insight, and he crosses the great divide as though walking in his sleep; he is in the process of conquering Paris. What interests us are his new Paris works. These are perhaps only three pictures: *Double Portrait, Portrait of the Artist's Wife,* and *The Bouquet.* You hear the titles? Back to simplicity, a tremendous step, especially for a Chagall. No more anecdotes, no poetic fancies, simply robust painting, taut classical discipline and the discovery of colour, the divine *odeur* in a picture. And look, here too Chagall achieves mastery at the first stroke! All at once he paints like a Frenchman, yet there is not a line of Ingres, not a dot of van Gogh. It is all Chagall – he paints with areas of colour and no longer with ideologies: that is the vast difference between Paris and the East. What no Cubist succeeded in doing he accomplished without effort and he stands among the first before the gates of the Louvre.'

In the *Double Portrait* referred to by Goll, Bella once more appears in a festal white dress. One has only to compare this white with that of the dress in the portrait of Bella with the black gloves of 1910 to feel how Chagall now sees white as a colour, even if – as also applies to the colours of a bouquet – it is still held captive by the precise contours of a form. The bouquet so much admired by Goll was more than merely one subject among many: the theme 'flowers' was to shine like a *leitmotiv* through Chagall's imagery during the years to come.

Chagall did not confine himself to Paris, as during the years 1910–1914; he felt the urge to get to know the French countryside, particularly that of the South. Henceforth he spent several months of the year on the Riviera, in Savoy, and at the foot of the Pyrenees, and he began to see the beauty of these landscapes with the eyes of the Impressionists. In the painting *My Daughter at the Window* (1924) we seek in vain for the first time the typical features of a Chagall picture. It lacks the arbitrary colouring, the flirting with Cubism, and allusions to Vitebsk. A young girl – Chagall's daughter Ida – sits on the window-sill looking out at the pastel-green of a mountain and the clouds in a summer sky. The paint is laid on with great sensitivity; for all their distinctness and verisimilitude the forms breathe the freshness of spontaneous experience. How rich are the blues and greens and the modulations of grey, a colour that had rarely appeared in Chagall's previous paintings. How charming is the contrast between the objects seen directly and those seen through the window, the two groups being held in equilibrium by the figure of the girl and the bouquet of sunflowers.

Chagall relates that he was first struck by the beauty of flowers during a visit to Toulon. He began to love bouquets of flowers for the diversity of the large and small blooms of which they were composed; he observed the scale of their variations in colour and form. Blossoms embedded in the cool blue-green of their foliage, the brilliant-coloured bouquet against the blue of the Mediterranean sky – Renoir and Odilon Redon had celebrated them before him: the first as a fervent glorifier of flesh tints, the second as a mystic seeking to penetrate the profound arcanum of colour. Chagall experienced in flowers the wonder of matter and what he called the 'chemistry' of colour.

Through an active immersion in the problems of painting and a hitherto unknown, grateful opening-up to nature, Chagall gained a new notion of reality, the gradual development of which may be traced in the pictures he painted during the next few years. This attention to the secrets which the visible world encloses in form and colour is not, of course, a variation of the realistic way of looking at things nor does it represent a renunciation of Chagall's perpetual endeavour to make manifest the 'fourth dimension'. 'I have sought to give concrete expression in a human fashion to man's powerlessness before nature. I have not tried to take revenge, but to strive after an output *(effort)* that runs parallel with nature's, if I may so express it…', he said in an interview recorded by Maurice Raynal.

These *efforts* gave rise to colours and values that were informed with a new life and 'surreal' significance. As in the evolution of periods of art – of Greek art, for instance – so in the development of the individual artist there often occurs a joyful moment when the soul itself finds expression in the aspect of people and things.

Chagall's earlier pictures were already filled with the mystery of that 'other element' which can always be felt when the creative impulses of the heart so permeate the artistic media that one becomes identical with the other. That the painter not only creates poetry, but at the same time awakens and brings into view the poetic core slumbering in beings, phenomena, objects, colours and forms – their inner soul – we have seen confirmed in every one of Chagall's works. Now we shall observe what happens when he seeks to refine his means, to put more and more life into his colours, to intensify his artistic self-expression, his own creative vigour, and not least his own mental powers, thereby releasing forces that contribute to a more comprehensive sort of poetry, which Raissa Maritain once described as 'une divination du spirituel dans le sensible'.

Our conception of Chagall's iconography will always involve the themes of idyllic love, of the happiness of lovers, and of soaring acrobats and angels. These various figures are all emanations of a single impulse – love. We have already noted the extent to which Chagall succeeds, in pictures celebrating the mystery of love, in combining an intimate confession with objective and poetic statement; we have seen how the one adds to the other, raising subjective experience into the realm of the miracle that is valid for everyone.

Yet Chagall's lovers change. In *The Birthday* begun in 1915, the colours and forms are still of picture-book simplicity. The soaring youth has neither arms nor hands. A wingless angel of the hour of love, he draws his yearning beloved up towards him by the force of his desire.

In *The Couple* (1928) the lovers exist in a different dimension of experience. In drawing and poetic conception it approaches, more than any earlier work by the artist, the picture of 'reality' transmitted by tradition, without any diminution of orginality and charm. Despite the duties which the use of these means lays upon him, Chagall succeeds in making the interpenetration of dream and daylight plausible, in rendering the earthly transcendent. The bodies have been given arms and hands that clasp and caress one another. The figures are caught in a mesh of leaves and flowers.

This painting resembles one that had been started earlier, *The Angel with the Palette* (1926–36). As in many of the earlier pictures and those still to come, the main line of composition is the diagonal. The diagonal is intermediate between the horizontal and the vertical; it is by nature a symbol of transition. The figures of the lovers are replaced by that of an angel, the foliage on either side of the figures by angel's wings. The angel of lovers, the beloved as an angel, and the angel as a muse – these beings anticipate the more powerful portrayals of angels belonging to a more tragic period in Chagall's creative life. As in Paul Klee's paintings, here too, we must avoid any attempt to interpret the angel theologically. Chagall would not understand any speculation as to the 'nature' of this angel. It changes from picture to picture, from the angel of the hour of love to the figure of flaming Lucifer, and always depends upon the hour and the encounter, of whose mystery it is the guardian and embodiment.

We have learnt how much Chagall's colour gains in aroma, how much more French his *peinture* becomes, in his 'flower period', that is to say the period following his second meeting with *la douce France*. If the houses, streets and fences of Vitebsk reappear or mingle with those of French villages in the pictures of this epoch, they, too, have become more dreamlike, more in the nature

of pure painting. The Chagallian animal – that creature which may be at once donkey, cow and goat – was displaced for a time by the circus horse in gala trappings, the dream horse of our childhood. It is accompanied by fairylike circus riders, harlequins and musicians in eighteenth century costume.
Degas, Seurat, Rouault, Picasso and Miró – they all loved and painted the world of the travelling people; each one of them saw embodied in this world and its inhabitants a fragment of his own world with its happiness and sorrow, its glory and misery.

'I have always regarded clowns, acrobats and actors as tragic figures, which for me resemble the figures in certain religious paintings', said Chagall. 'I did not want to spare any of the more moving, tender feelings in a picture of a clown or a circus rider, feelings which one would experience in painting a madonna, a Christ, a rabbi with the Torah, or a pair of lovers. One could even enlarge this idea and say that a so-called "subject" (although I dislike the expression) should not, in fact, exactly resemble that which it intends to express, but rather make an allusion to something else in order to achieve that resemblance.'
The riders, acrobats and clowns live in a realm where the laws of gravity, space and time no longer apply. Eccentric behaviour is for them natural, the expression of their existence and nature. Thus the harlequins in the mural in the Moscow Jewish Theatre performed handstands in mid-air, an acrobat in a 1924 etching danced on an upright violin. In a picture of 1927 we see a circus horse balancing on a sphere and on the same sphere a clown with an umbrella – an equilibristic monstrosity in which only the painter and his means of expression are in balance. The colour shares in the secret of this balance, it makes these visions credible, however much the legs of the riders and the horses bend and stretch in contradiction of every anatomical law, however far the heads of the clowns stretch ecstatically towards the sky. In the gouaches of this period the colour joins in the jubilant spectacle of the circus folk. With a little green and blue, and a touch of carmine and Naples yellow, their creator conjures up a whirling, singing rococo conformation of dabs, splodges and spirals that coagulate – as though in response to music – into forms and outlines, hold them for a moment, and next instant regroup themselves in fresh configurations.
Among these works, many of which resemble décors for a dream theatre, are some in which expression, form and poetic content reach a level of the greatest beauty. Two pictures awaken the delight of those who, in a world of anxiety and pain, long for the consolation of unspoilt charm. These are *The Girl Acrobat* (1930), which hangs in the Musée d'Art Moderne, Paris, and the *Lovers on a Horse* or *The Circus Riders* (1931), now in the possession of the Municipal Museum, Amsterdam.

Above the patina-encrusted, intercalated buildings and a huge Romanesque church door glimmers an enamelled sky. The architectural sections might have been painted by Monet. One feels the age stored up in them, the warmth trembling behind their surfaces. In front of this background, filling the whole area of the picture, floats the girl acrobat, half sitting, half leaning against the thin tilted bar of the trapeze. The silk fleshings in which the figure is clad are a festal pink. The feet are shod in red dancing shoes and crossed as though in a ballet step. From the low neckline rise a pair of spotless shoulders, a throat with a pearl necklace, and the oval of a quietly smiling face with enquiring eyes. This face – a tender variation on the two heads in the *Birthday* picture – resembles the profile of the husband floating down from the clouds.

The same magical power distinguishes the second of these two paintings. Here the soft brightness of the paint and the *sfumato* of the brushwork recall the most precious enamel-painting. The lovers float past in a close embrace mounted on a white horse. The girl is of flowerlike loveliness, the posture of her body and limbs full of amorous charm. The background consists of the flocculent *grisaille* of the night sky. In front of these grey-white pastel shades blossoms once more the pink of the circus costume, that leaves the girl's soft breasts bare. A red flower in her indigo-coloured, full hair adds to the festal character of the hour; the triangle of the fan above the horse's head sparkles like a mounted ruby. The young man's jerkin is a rich, velvety green. The bent head of the horse has a visionary quality: this is how we have always imagined Lancelot's horse or Bayard's. Carefully, as though aware of the preciousness of its burden, the horse holds under its chin a rose-wreathed violin. Its eyes are only touched in as almost imperceptible shadows beneath the silky mane that falls down over its forehead. It needs no eyes to bear these riders, who are not bound for any destination.
The texture of the embroidery in the pink of the dress and the ornamentation on the silver-grey saddlecloth are particularly finely painted. In the background a faint crossbar is visible bearing the outline of a violinist. In the right-hand lower corner, as though seen from a bird's eye view, is a group of strange musicians: a clown is playing a violin, while a seated blue cow and a cock sing, and a second clown dreamily performs the steps and gestures of a soundless dance . . .
'The circus is a tiny closed off arena of forgetfulness', says Henry Miller in his story of clowns, *The Smile at the Foot of the Ladder*. 'For a space it enables us to lose ourselves, to dissolve in wonder and bliss, to be transported by the mystery . . . A clown is a poet in action. He is the story he enacts. It is the same story over and over – adoration, devotion, crucifixion. A "Rosy Crucifixion", *bien entendu*.'

It must have been a fascinating undertaking to compare Chagall's circus figures with Picasso's. A Paris critic wrote at the time: 'As though heaven wished to exhaust all its miracles at once, Picasso and Chagall appeared to us at the same time. Picasso's art has a tragic inhumanity, one cannot believe that life can exist in this world which he has invented in every detail. Chagall, on the other hand, is the oriental magician who transforms the most commonplace aspects of life into a fairyland. In his pictures the city of Toulon becomes a village where the heroes of Hans Andersen's stories live happily ever after. A feeling for the fantastic is entirely alien to the French mind. Of all countries, France is the one whose painting makes the least demands on the imagination. Where is our Rembrandt, our Fra Angelico? This explains the resistance Chagall has often encountered in Paris. Only yesterday the success *The Girl Acrobat* enjoyed in the Salon des Tuileries by virtue of its strangeness prevented many people from also acknowledging the picture's painterly qualities, so long has the prejudice of *peinture pure* survived among us.'

Meanwhile Jacques Maritain hailed the latest works of his friend – whom he compared, in his love for man and beast, with St Francis – as a 'happy disaster', necessary so that men might regain their faith in the miracle of freedom and the innocence of the world despite the devil's horns that were beginning to show everywhere.

All the pictures Chagall had painted since his return from Russia were joyfully recapitulated in the painting *The Lovers in the Lilacs*, dated 1931 and now in America.

Before a night sky of cloudy blue a gigantic bunch of lilac is flowering in a vase that is washed by the waters of a river spanned by a bridge. In the midst of the bunch, in a nest of pink, white and mauve blossoms, the lovers lie pressed close together, shyly alert, as though listening to a music that is not of this world. The clothes of the youth are purple, like the shadows on the green leaves; the shadows on the body of his sweetheart are the same mysterious colour. The veil-like skirt that clings round the girl's body from the hips resembles a mermaid's scales. Her limbs, flexible as a dancer's, recall those of the acrobat, only her element is not the immensity of the night sky, but the fathomless iridescent ocean of the flowers, through which she glides like a naiad.

The clouds in the sky are reflected in the shadows of the lilac blossoms, the moons of the girl's breasts compete in mystery with the mystery of the real moon and its image mirrored in the river. 'With this picture', said one critic, 'Chagall has achieved with the rays of the moon an effect comparable to the effect of sunlight in the work of the Impressionists.'

At the very moment when Parisian critics were hailing Chagall's new pictorial world as an enrichment of the 'Ecole de Paris', a fresh event occurred to astound them – an exhibition of a hundred gouaches illustrating *The Fables of La Fontaine*, which Vollard held at the Galerie Bernheim-Jeune in February 1930.
Chagall had not yet finished the plates for *Dead Souls* when Vollard invited him to design a series of colour engravings for the fables of the classical French poet and moralist. This project may have been suggested to the publisher by one of the Gogol etchings, in which grunting, cackling and crowing farmyard animals are holding a lively and picturesque meeting within an encircling fence. The gouaches were intended as preliminary sketches for the engravings. Vollard had a studio built and obtained the services of the famous artisan-engraver Maurice Potin and a team of skilled workmen, who were to translate the gouaches into engravings under Chagall's supervision.
The exhibition of gouaches, however, was more than a display of sketches for the forthcoming illustrations; it proved to be a collection of a hundred works that were masterpieces in their own right. Every one of them radiated a gaiety that did not spring merely from the theme; the colours and forms, the whole composition, were gay. The sickle of the moon, the waves in the river, the outlines of the clouds, all the dashes, patches and splashes of paint, smile just as much as the faces of the fables' heroes — the wolf, the stork, the lion and the sheep. Even the coachman threatened by a storm and the ox collapsing under the shaft of the hay-waggon that has run into a bog are smiling. They exhibit all the merriment that actors in a Molière play bring to his tragi-comic scenes, where everyone knows that it is all a joke, a dream in broad daylight. And if the spectator grows serious when the raised forefinger comes into view – the next instant his meditative mood is brushed away by fresh capers.
The comic genius requires to be nourished by ever fresh constellations of ideas. This is wholly true of Chagall's hundred gouaches: every sheet differs from the rest in the originality of its plastic charm. Chagall's illustrations also have their moral. But to the pleasure of seeing La Fontaine's *Fables* interpreted in a new way, of coming across new and hitherto unrealized beauties that were latent in them, is added the delight of enjoying a piece of fine painting.
The grapes gleam with humidity and sweetness, and the fox's fur bristles with greed. Grass and water, the sky and the foliage of the trees, the material of clothes and other everyday objects are all solid and tangible, fragrant and pliant, pleasant or repulsive – like the perpetually changing phenomena of nature. As soon as we take it in, we are astounded by the miraculous wealth of colours in

VI *The Bride and Groom of the Eiffel Tower, 1938-39*

which the painter has clothed his vision. These gouaches, like so many of his earlier works, look as though they had been created in response to a joyful impulse; yet anyone who has watched Chagall at work knows how cautiously he proceeds, how carefully he keeps check on every stage of the picture's development, how he experiments and at the same time incorporates each new discovery, with unerring instinct, in the creative process. One cannot tell whether the painting hand is guided by the greatest alertness and attention, or whether its movements testify to a somnambulistic certainty that causes every trace of effort to disappear and be forgotten. Here, too, the facility we marvel at is a result and not a precondition. In these works we are once more struck by the absence of the pathos that so easily appears in the train of mannerism, but at the same time the painter's handwriting is as 'Chagallian' as ever.

To Chagall the fables and their morals are only a medium. Since he knows the animals and the world in which they live, and the people they personify, and since, moreover, he is a painter of the first rank, he reduces the literary element in his illustrations to a minimum and achieves an immediate cathartic moral effect by purely pictorial means: the spectator looks at the picture, allows himself to be bewitched by its poetry – and smiles, even if he has long ago forgotten the fable that gave rise to it.

Despite all the qualities revealed by the Bernheim-Jeune exhibition, many critics were worried. Since they had to admit the merits of the pictures as *morceaux de peinture*, they tried to justify their critical displeasure on other, less earnest, grounds. 'How can this oriental and romantic illustrate our classical poet?' they cried. 'The very idea is paradoxical.' Vollard intervened personally in the debate. He pointed out that La Fontaine himself had drawn many of the themes for his fables, together with their atmosphere and poetic conception, from oriental tales and legends, so that they contained a considerable non-French element. He informed the critics that the famous Russian fabulist Krylov, whose fables are known to every Russian child and whose lines have become household words, had translated La Fontaine's fables. He told them it had been his wish to find an artist who was familiar, by virtue of his origin, with the magic of the East and capable of translating the fables into a visual equivalent. 'If I am asked: Why Chagall?' this explanation goes on, ' I reply: Precisely because his aesthetic seems to me close to La Fontaine's and in a way related to it, firm and gentle, at once realistic and fantastic.'

Meanwhile, work on the colour engravings was not going well, despite repeated experiments. After many technical failures Vollard commissioned Chagall to produce colour etchings. But these did not satisfy him either. The plates were again destroyed and the decision was finally reached to have black and white

etchings. All this trouble was recompensed by the final result: the etchings were in no way inferior to the gouaches in their wealth of ideas and graphic solidity. His attempts to produce colour etchings impelled Chagall to strive after the same effects in black and white as he had previously aimed at with the use of colour.

There were also approving voices – that of the poet Philippe Soupault for example. His appraisal is all the more valuable because he had an opportunity of watching the painter at work and following the development of the etchings. 'When Chagall etches he bends low over his work and examines it very closely, the details gain importance. Thus on one plate, one of those that immediately grip and enchant us, we see a forest in the background. Thousands of little trees that are in reality innumerable small twigs. This plate, which proves how much importance Chagall attached to details, also testifies to his desire to give the whole picture unity, creating such a powerful atmosphere that it seems to take us by the throat when the plate is pulled. And then this forest, which at first glance seems to lie in the distance, moves closer and comes to meet our eyes. Soon it occupies the whole area and spills over out of it . . ., it is alive.'
'We cannot, as one usually does with etchings', Soupault continues, 'simply admire the fineness of the details or the relationship of the plastic values. Chagall teaches us, over and above this, to love, desire and demand an atmosphere that emanates from these lines, these white and black areas. Chagall never loses contact with reality, but it must be said that he eludes reality, the reality we are accustomed to think of as unalterable. A man who greets (or a landscape that embraces a wide tract of country) has a double face. Anyone who sees therein only the immediate effect, who seeks in a drawing only something he can look at, will completely fail to notice the sound it emits – if we may so express it – this sound that awakens the echoes of a deeper reality. And the very thing to be marvelled at in these etchings is the resonance, the reflexions, that radiate from them . . .'

Rembrandt

Chagall finished the etchings for *The Fables of La Fontaine* in 1931. Shortly afterwards Vollard commissioned him to do a series of etchings illustrating the Old Testament. It is difficult to imagine how this idea arose and how Vollard planned to print and publish the work. Both *Dead Souls* and the *Fables* were published by Tériade long after Vollard's death. The Bible illustrations took even longer, and Chagall worked on them for more than twenty years.

Perhaps Vollard considered it his duty to encourage Chagall to undertake this work; long experience with painters had taught him that even in these days the artist who draws his inspiration entirely from within himself needs commissions, which, under certain circumstances, may first give him freedom for artistic self-realization. The plan to have Chagall do the illustrations for his projected edition of the Bible shows Vollard's confidence in Chagall and his insight into the essential nature of Chagall's art. Just as, in the face of hostile criticism, he considered Chagall capable of illustrating the fables of the 'Bonhomme', so he now entrusted to him a task that reached down into the deepest zone of religious experience.

Chagall began the preliminary work on this cycle with journeys to countries and pictures from which he hoped to gain insight into the spirit of the Jewish world and its artistic Portrayal. These journeys took him to Palestine, where he observed people and landscapes, to Spain, where he examined the work of El Greco, and finally to Holland, where he studied the world of Rembrandt.

Rembrandt has always moved people who see in him and his work the embodiment of their longings, sufferings and joys, who are drawn to him by more than purely artistic interest. The artists of this period, who sought to evolve and solve the problems of their painting solely out of the laws of *peinture* did not feel greatly attracted to Rembrandt. With him 'they were not on the last rung of the spirit, where strange things are created that are at once the method and object of knowledge' (Jean Cassou).

In Rembrandt's work life is condensed into art, every stroke of the brush presupposes a human impulse springing equally from passionate adoration of the earthly and a striving after knowledge of the divine. He has bared his heart to us in dozens of self-portraits. It is therefore no wonder that those painters chose Rembrandt as a model for whom logic and clarity were not the ultimate goal of art and who were more concerned to bring their daemonic and apocalyptic visions into harmony with the media of art – such artists as Odilon Redon, Ensor, Soutine and Rouault. Quite different again was Picasso's attitude to the northern genius; in Rembrandt, as in van Gogh, he must have been gripped solely by the 'human drama and turmoil'. Chagall's love for Rembrandt, on the other hand, has roots which the biographers of modern painting do not mention nowadays because they seem to them to lie outside the domain of art. These roots are their common peasant origin, the significance which family life and early environment had for both painters, the glorification of the beloved, the urge to depict themselves in every new metamorphosis, the Jewish element in the iconography of both of them, the profound religious sense which, in both instances, led away from dogma to a message that was addressed to all mankind. Then there was their exaltation of matter as it appears to the painter, their realization that the world is in a state of darkness in which objects shine forth through the power of their being, and the realism that is determined by their own experience and always remains the foundation of their mystical revelations. Finally, both of them see drawing as an element of life; Rembrandt, too, never set down a line or a 'tone' that does not bear the stamp of experience.

The facial expression Rembrandt put into the portrait of his friend the Amsterdam Rabbi Menasseh ben Israel, and the prophetic wisdom in the countenance of the father in the picture of the return of the prodigal son – which Chagall once studied in the Hermitage – naturally differ from the expression of Chagall's rabbis, just as the forms of the painting of those days, and the age that produced them, differed. And yet we can see today the affinity between the two creations, the melancholy that is fed from the same sources, the kindliness that rises above their painful experience of the world.

Chagall would object to his work being compared to that of an El Greco, a Tintoretto or a Rembrandt. For him, too, these geniuses embody Parnassus – more unattainable today than ever before. Thus he did not study Rembrandt in order to learn from him a manner, a recipe, as those painters still hope to do who copy his *Man with the Golden Helmet*. His quest is always for the origin, 'for the spirit of the fathers and grandfathers, their essential being', a striving 'to commune with them . . ., with their souls and sorrows, their troubles and their rare joys'.

Etchings for the Bible

In 1934, when the first forty etchings for the Bible were shown in Paris, Jacques Maritain wrote in *Les Cahiers d'Art:*

'To illustrate the Bible was a unique test of Chagall's art. This test has been to the artist's advantage. He has renewed himself and yet remained true to himself. In limitation and concentration his art, laying aside the active aggressiveness of colour, all the more successfully reveals the human and poetic quality, the depth of feeling, which renders it so dear to us. Abstractly – eliminating the activity of the brain – he guides the etching needle independently of any method, following the example of the old masters. An inventive technique, dictated by an alert sensibility, miraculously causes the black and white to sing, and black in black, with subtle modulations, like the chanting in a synagogue. The living phenomena that rise from the depths like the gestures of tired hands, and beg for pity, grow out of a kind of fluid chaos that has furrowed the soul. At the same time greatness also appears – as in the descent of the angels with Abraham, the surging solitude of Moses, or the marvellous Creation of Man that is so noble in its movements...'

Looking at these prints – of which there were finally over a hundred, every one of them revealing mysteries that go far beyond the purely artistic and aesthetic sphere – the spectator is led into the silence of a vanished world; and yet the objects, figures, animals and landscapes that inhabit it are made poetically present to him. The imagery of the Bible has always aroused corresponding images in our dreams and preoccupied our imaginations. But just as imagination is fed by the experience man acquires in daily contact with his environment, so the pictures conjured up by the Bible draw their substance from our memories of the earth.

It can happen, too, that we recognize as 'biblical' a real landscape, a human figure in a particular attitude and setting, an animal whose pose suggests all the humility of the creature: the vine- and olive-clad hills of Provence, girls walking in the cool of evening with their great jugs to the well in an Italian village, a weary ass in the shade of a mulberry tree, emaciated lamenting women wrapped in black shawls sitting in front of chalky white cemetery walls somewhere in Crete... These scenes prove that life itself at certain moments may assume the dimensions of the hallowed and allegorical, that biblical images slumber in our consciousness, only waiting to be aroused or – in the language of the artist – given form. There can be no doubt that these flashes of recognition are not due solely to the physical aspect of what we see, but that we project something of our own dreams and fantasies on to the scenery and figures.

In the moments when such encounters take place, the world loses its normal proportions and casts aside the fetters laid upon it by space and time and conventional experience. It has always been the poets – and with them the painters – who have disclosed the secret meaning of these revelations, and presented it to us in the shape of powerful visual images.

In his etchings for the Bible, Chagall proves himself such a poet, resembling the great primitives, who 'under the assault of their inner world, spontaneously abstracted from the natural universe forms of inexhaustible significance' (Raissa Maritain).

For the sake of these encounters Chagall visited the countryside of Palestine and Egypt, in which these hallowed events took place. 'In the East I found the Bible and part of my own being. The air of the Land of Israel makes one wise', he said on his return.

This wisdom speaks from the etchings, a wisdom which, despite all its penetration and profundity, is kindly and often even jovial. Although every print is rich in formal artistic problems, the element of subjective ratiocination – such as we see, for example, in Kokoschka's illustrations for the Bible – is absent; and they are free from the dogmatic transfiguration of suffering that is expressed in Rouault's *Miserere* engravings. Yet the silent drama in the faces of Chagall's lamenting and sorrowing prophets – those scenes in which suffering permeates every element of the picture – remain unforgettable. No one can remain indifferent to the bowed figure of Jacob, transformed by the news of Joseph's death into a monument to grief. But this suffering takes place in an atmosphere steeped in the omnipresent mercy of God, so that we feel no temptation to self-tormenting identification with the sufferer.

To the deep, majestic notes of the formal, pictorial elements are added the clear, high tones of lyrical devotion. The etching of Abraham's meeting with the three angels has the quality of a folk-tale and an infinite sweetness and innocence of style. Another print, showing Rebekah and the servant at the well, is bright with an altogether earthly light. Equally earthly is the figure of young Joseph as a shepherd; the goat at his side wears the same look of purity and innocence. Chagall's prophets and angels have a human quality, and his ordinary men and women dream under the protection of a good and loving father. The ingenuousness with which Chagall portrays his characters and creatures enables him even to introduce the figure of the artist himself without destroying the picture's plausibility – as in the etching of the Creation of Man, where God hastens down to earth with the sleeping Adam in his arms. The artlessness that moves us here is in strange contrast to the intelligence that shines through the use of pictorial means and touches us in a different zone of our sensibility. And yet artlessness and intelligence form a unity, a unity in which innocence is not a preliminary but a result. Thus we can apprehend the hallowed and hallowing quality of Chagall's etchings as something born from the sum total of all his efforts, as the poetic mystery come to life – a mystery which may ultimately be religious in character. The artistic constituents of his etchings also tremble and vibrate with this mysterious life: luminosity is more than an optical phenomenon, darkness is full of unfathomable depths, configurations undergo perpetual metamorphoses. Cloud-shadows, rocks, foliage and garments are forever changing into faces, angels' wings, and eyes.

Time is a River without Banks

On a picture of 1931, bearing the title *Winter,* we see once more the pendulum clock that we have already met in a pen drawing of his parents' living-room at Vitebsk and in a painting of 1915; in the latter it appears motionless as a still life, dominating a grey interior wall, at the lower end of which young Marc is sitting, gazing out of a window. Is it, then, a property out of the treasure-house of youth – like the lamp, the mirror, the plate with the fish – and, like these, steeped in symbolic significance?

VII *King David*, *1950–51*

On the 1931 picture the old-fashioned clock-case flies along upright with one wing extended, filling the area of a snow-covered village square. Footprints in the snow lead to three wooden houses, like the house in which Chagall spent his childhood. The gable of the carved, mahogany-coloured clock bears the same cap of snow as the roofs of the houses. The clockface is at the same time the head of a female nude that has been magically imprisoned inside the clock-case. The wing might belong to this nude. To the left of the clock – perhaps it is the shadow of time – floats an oval of transparent blue.

Clocks, clock hands, hour figures and pendulums also occur in the paintings of the Surrealists, especially those of Salvador Dali and Max Ernst; Paul Klee makes use of them as enigmatic ciphers. These painters must have been attracted more by the clock as a symbol of time, of change and decay, of perpetual motion, than by its picturesque outward appearance. Are the clocks in Chagall's pictures likewise media for philosophical commentaries in paint, codes to be deciphered as a psychoanalyst deciphers the symbols of a dream, which, as we know, represent unconscious impulses in disguise? The poet, like the child, sees phenomena in all their uninterpreted magic. Kierkegaard recalls that when he was a boy a patch of green paint on a wall seemed to him a message from the 'other world'. If we were to translate the painter's symbols into the everyday language of the understanding, his efforts at 'poeticization' would have been in vain. We must, rather, leave the incomprehensible in its state of mystery, we must abandon ourselves to it until its message reaches us and we become one with it.

We can imagine what the clock must have meant to Chagall as a child, when he dreamed about objects, people and events in the house in Pokrovskaya Street and, among all the familiar things in the room, something moved like a living creature that had hands and numbers and a bell inside it and that was connected, for the adults, with something called 'time', which the boy could not understand. Later, recollection of the clock must have been linked up with the other symbols of flux and flow – water, birds, fishes, and one's pulse-beat that becomes terrifyingly perceptible at moments of joy and fear.

It may be objected that we are dealing with pictures, and not with the psychological interpretation of childhood experiences. But the aims and effects of poetry are inseparable from personal biography. We have already seen that elements in a picture which, at first sight, appear strange, may be the source of subtle radiations that lift the picture on to a plane of truer and more significant expression.

This is what Paul Reverdy means by his famous dictum concerning the 'image': 'The image is a pure creation of the mind. It cannot be engendered by a simile, but only by bringing together two more or less disparate realities... An image is not powerful because it is violent or fantastic – but because the association of ideas is remote and correct... A powerful image, new to the mind, is created by bringing together without a simile two remote realities, whose connexion with one another has been apprehended only by the mind...'

Time is a River without Banks. This saying, which comes from Ovid, Chagall used as the title of a painting on which he worked from 1930 to 1939. Again a clock goes sailing through the air, this time leaning to one side. The brass frame of the blank clockface and the pendulum gleams through the glass. In defiance of the laws of gravity, the pendulum is swinging towards the uppermost side. The woodwork of the clock is painted in loving detail. The clock hangs down from the body of a fish, whose splendid garment of scales glitters with the green, yellow and blue of Bengal fire. Mighty pinions grow out of its back, but they are more like huge fins than feathered wings. An arm projects from the fish's mouth, holding in its hand a violin and a bow.

The background consists of a twilight-blue river landscape – almost the same as the one in *The Lovers in the Lilacs* – with river-banks, houses, a church, a distant bridge, and a boat sailing on the water. The movement of the paint forming the sky follows the contours of the fish's wings. The front right-hand bank is occupied along its whole length by a pair of lovers sinking down in a passionate embrace, over whom the violet shadows of the bank break like a wave.

In this picture motion and immobility, time and timelessness, flux and stillness, passion and the peace of the soul, are united in a harmony of colour and form. The painting is a visual equivalent of Hugo von Hofmannsthal's enigmatic dictum: 'And three are one: a man, a thing, a dream.'

Before this painting the spectator becomes aware of a new note that henceforth rings out of Chagall's pictures, a restrained melancholy and a poetic wisdom, Wordsworth's 'still, sad music of humanity' that characterizes every great work of art. This note is audible in *The Violinist in the Snow* (1931), in which a bearded old man dressed in blue-green, occupying the whole width of the picture, soars across the snow-covered foreground of a street lined with houses. His countenance is full of sorrow. With his hands he crushes to his breast a violin and bow – his sole remaining consolation. Two years later, in 1933, Chagall painted *Solitude.* The left-hand side of the picture is taken up by a seated rabbi, his face and body enveloped in a white prayer-shawl. His right hand supports his bowed head, his left holds a huge Torah scroll. Beside this solitary figure sunk in profound melancholy is the incarnation of peace and gentleness in the shape of a reclining white cow, which is once more accompanied by a violin and a bow as symbolic attributes. The sky over Vitebsk is rent by lightning, through the clouds soars an angel bearing a message.

In 1934 Chagall painted *The Bride's Chair,* on the occasion of his daughter Ida's wedding. It is a picture in white with a little pink and pale green. The background consists of the window-wall of a room got up for the feast; between the long white curtains stands a white-covered arm chair surrounded by a blaze of roses, which also climb up from the seat of the chair. A pink carpet on the gleaming floor enhances the festal effect. Paintings by Chagall hang on the walls; in the background stands a table bearing candlesticks and flowers. This picture keeps to perspective in the drawing, which gives it an especially high degree of 'reality'. It might have been painted by Bonnard. But Chagall does not rest content with a festive harmony of colours: he penetrates into the substance of the colours and transforms surface charm into true painting. The truths that lie behind appearances are also perceptible – the ambergris odour of decay, the end of all worldly beauty. The crossbar of the window frame stands out in the flood of white like a *memento mori* in the hour of happiness.

A presentiment of coming events hangs over the lovers in *The Three Candles* (1938). The couple soar through the air in a close embrace. The bride's head, in a white veil, leans on the shoulder of the man. But his head is turned down towards the three burning candles in the bottom left hand corner of the picture. Again the couple are soaring beneath the shadow of an enormous bouquet of flowers, through which fly cherubim and musicians. An angel holds the border of a white shawl that envelops the two lovers. The reclining cow, the flute-playing harlequin on the fence, the jubilant people in the streets, the synagogues – all are wrapped in innocence, as though things would always remain like this. And yet forebodings of the future make us tremble like the lovers.

We meet the same lovers in a picture, *A ma femme,* that was begun in 1934 and not completed until 1944, and which now hangs in the Musée d'Art Moderne, Paris. In this painting we find all the attributes of Chagall's pictorial world gathered together into a *concerto grosso* – the wedding canopy, the bouquets of flowers, the winged clock, the fish and the cock, the violin-playing Uncle Neuch, the cow, the bunch of purple lilac; and amongst them all, like a miraculous blossom, Bella herself. The background is indigo blue – recalling the dark patina'd glass in a cathedral window – out of which the stronger chromatic accents flash and sparkle like amethysts, rubies and emeralds. The houses also have faces, and the folds of the curtains, which open on to the spectacle of Chagall's visions, once more disclose lauding angels. This picture might easily be split up into a number of separate paintings, each one capable of standing on its own as an independent work of art. It is all the more astonishing, therefore, how the painter has tied these individual scenes together by means of colour and composition. We still feel something of Cubism's rhythms of space and colour and Delaunay's Orphic *simultané.* But the spatial tensions have more soul, more of a dreamlike quality, the graphic elements are still more of a living structure, the lines pulse like arteries beneath the breathing epidermis of the paint. The felicitous pictorial metaphors do not conceal the extent to which they are the outcome of painful experiences and insights.

The *Cello Player* of 1939 is animated by the same solemn dignity. Here, too, the colours gleam like the pieces of a stained glass window. The player, a two-faced Orpheus, *is* the instrument from which he is drawing music, and the houses of Vitebsk, this time quite close to the foreground, are the walls of Thebes that amplified his song. The singer's hair waves like a golden flame against the cerulean blue of the sky, in which leaves that glisten like turquoises are whirling. The roofs and snow-covered houses glimmer in the rays of the full moon. On a chair sits the Chagallian animal, dressed in a suit and likewise playing a violin, gazing adoringly up at the great glorifier, whose head is adorned with a crown as a sign of his princely dignity. This work carried Chagall into the circle of the prophets among modern European painters. Only a poet's words are apposite to convey the fervour of this painting. 'Is he of this world? No, out of the two worlds grew his broad nature', sings Rilke in his *Sonnet to Orpheus.* And at the beginning of one of his last poems we find the words: *Bestürz mich, Musik, mit rhythmischem Zürnen!... Die Wölbungen warten, dass du sie füllst mit orgelndem Andrang...,* and *Hat deine Sehnsucht nicht Atem, aus der Posaune des Engels, der das Weltgericht anbricht, tönende Stürme zu stossen...?* 'Dumbfound me, music, with rhythmical anger!... The vaults, the highest, are waiting for you to fill them with the rushing notes of an organ...'; 'Has thy longing not breath to draw echoing storms from the trumpets of the angel who announces the Day of Judgement...?'

Apocalypse of the Soul

While he was working on the etchings for the Bible and the pictures of the Twenties and Thirties, there stood in the various studios Chagall occupied during this period an uncompleted work which he had begun in 1923 and was not to finish until twenty-five years later. This painting was *The Falling Angel,* which bears the dates 1923-33-47.

We have already noted that Chagall did not pass through any development in the sense of a changing series of styles – such as may be seen in the work of Picasso or Matisse – but merely shows an ever-increasing poetic density. If, with the aim of demonstrating Chagall's 'development' towards an ever more comprehensive poetic concentration, I have frequently tried to trace a painting back to the one that preceded it, this was solely for the purpose of bringing the poetic substance of the pictures into clearer view by comparison. Nothing would be more out of place than an attempt to trace a chronological sequence in this painter's creative evolution. Chagall's paintings, on which he often worked for decades, cannot be fitted into a chronological scheme. The causality in the 'evolution' of Chagall's art can no more be apprehended rationally than the logic of each individual picture. Chagall's creative impetus was fed precisely by the desire to break free from the bonds that tie us to the outworn criteria of reason in our thinking and feeling. 'The logical meaning has been, so to speak, swallowed up by the poetic, it has become dissolved and homeless and continues to exist only as a kind of motley substance for the poetic sense to work upon. The poetic sense is the only lantern in the darkness', we read in Jacques Maritain. Bearing this in mind, it is only with some hesitation that I shall attempt to describe *The Falling Angel.* This magnificently conceived work may be taken as typical of those visionary and foreboding paintings we have been considering. Half the picture is filled by the figure of the red angel hurtling head over heels earthward with outspread wings against a background of dark blue, indigo, purple and black, colours that flow into and over each other or bound one another like clouds or mountains in the intricate landscapes of our dreams.

The centre of the picture is occupied by the angel's face with the terrifying white eye, round which everything else passionately revolves. Each separate area of the surface, which is filled with all the attributes we know from earlier works, breathes an intense agitation. From the left-hand bottom corner rises the figure of an angry rabbi with a face of transparent blue, clad in a velvety purple *kaftan.* He holds in his arms an open Torah scroll. In the area above his head a crouching Russian peasant in an ultramarine jerkin is seeking to support himself with a stick as he falls through bright prismatic clouds. He is looking fearfully towards the monstrous angel who is falling with him. At the rabbi's side the horned 'animal' anxiously raises its yellow head. Its mouth touches a bright blue violin which seems to be playing itself with the bow that lies across it. Between the angel's face and the head of the rabbi and the animal glides the moon with an orange corona. In contrast to all this movement, the background of the right-hand bottom edge of the picture shows snow-covered Vitebsk in the still of the night, seen from above. From its roofs a female figure wearing a bride's veil and clasping a child rises into the angel's flaming wing, and in the village square stands a patina-green candlestick holding a candle that burns with a steady flame surrounded by a greenish halo. Against a background of red flames rising on the horizon towers a crucifix with the body of Christ shimmering pale lilac.

In the angel's uppermost wing we once more find the clock, and in the pallid mist of wintery Vitebsk at the bottom of the picture wanders the familiar Jew with a sack on his back.
The staggering new element in this painting is the Lucifer-like figure of the angel and the more or less traditional conception of Christ, who is, however, seen as thoroughly Jewish with a striped prayer shawl draped round his loins and the *tefillim*, the prayer-thongs, encircling his head.
Like the painting *A ma femme*, *The Falling Angel* may be divided into sections, into four major spheres of action, each of which possesses its own source of illumination, the central point round which it revolves. These discs – the moon, the clockface, the flame of the candle, and the halo of Christ – are planets in the greater cosmos of the picture as a whole.
The different parts of the picture are held together by two great curves of colour: the cool curve of blue and violet hues, and the curve with a red chromatic scale. At the same time, the specific note of each individual colour is fully felt.
The striking fact about this painting is the boldness with which these complexes of strongly contrasting colours are integrated into a tense and vital whole, into that 'apocalypse of the soul' which – according to Keats – is the expression of all poetry.
The logic pervading the picture's component parts becomes clear when we consider that a slight alteration in the tone-values, in the composition, or in the subject matter, would utterly destroy its beauty. What would the angel's wing be without the mother and child woven into it? What would the animal's head be without the violin and bow, the crucifixion without the candle that illumines it? There can hardly be anything like it in the whole of modern painting: this picture is neither surrealist nor allegorical, neither religiously determined nor the product of uncontrollable hallucination, neither realistic nor abstract: it is the outcome of powerful poetic vision, an example of truly authentic painting, a real Chagall, who with this creation comes very close to the works of the great whom he so much admires – Rembrandt, Grünewald and Goya.

Crucifixion – Martyrdom

1938. The drama Chagall had foreseen had become a reality. The Spanish Civil War with its terrors proved to be a bloody prelude to a still more frightful catastrophe. Picasso painted the turbulent visions of his mural, *Guernica*, out of passionate sympathy for the fate of his own homeland.
In Germany the anti-Jewish pogroms were raging, the concentration camps

were filling, innocent people were being tortured and killed, synagogues were going up in flames. As an answer to the appalling vistas which these days opened up for Chagall the artist, the man and the Jew, he painted *White Crucifixion*. From the harlequin to the Crucified! Chagall's artistic path was beginning to reach the fulfilment it had foreshadowed at the beginning.

The Christ of *White Crucifixion* is no longer in physical pain. He hangs motionless on the cross; the presence of this figure of suffering in the midst of a world that has broken all bounds is a symbol of inexorably fulfilled prophecy. In this bowed head with the closed eyes, the now silent prophet, who has offered himself up as a martyr, waits until the world – in accordance with Messianic prophecy – has exhausted itself in sin and suffering and become ripe for the promised Kingdom of God.

In this picture the synagogue is in flames, the ritual objects are scattered about the street, a Torah scroll is blazing, and the houses of the village have been hurled this way and that by the storm of destruction. Their inhabitants lie dead in the street or flee to all four points of the compass. A few are trying to escape in a boat; one group floats lamenting in the sky above a cross bearing in Hebrew letters the words 'Jesus of Nazareth, King of the Jews'. From the horizon the horde of Baal-worshippers come storming down with their murderous weapons and banners.

Chagall's Vitebsk was once tangible reality experienced and suffered; in the early pictures documentary fact and its poetic transfiguration were one. In the course of time this scenery became more and more a dream, a recollection, a vision painfully conjured up. In these new pictures the streets and houses of Chagall's birthplace regain their vivid actuality, with the result that the Vitebsk theme attains an unparalleled fusion of the present and the timeless.

The cross with the white body of Christ in the beam of light once more raises Chagall's iconography into a new dimension of artistic expression. It is no coincidence that the ray of light that streams down from the sky on to the earth ends in the halo round the flames of the Jewish candlestick at the foot of the cross. Again the accessories of Jewish religious ritual, the phylactery and the prayer shawl, are assigned to the figure of Christ. It might be tempting to interpret the connexion of these attributes with the figure of Christ from a historical or theological standpoint; but this would add nothing to the artistic content of the painting. Since Chagall does not feel himself an orthodox Jew, it would be inappropriate to explain the presence of the *tefillim* in this painting in terms of the orthodox Jew's image of himself. Chagall, the friend of Jacques and Raissa Maritain, sees the figure of Christ as the great poets see it: as the merciful Saviour of whom it is written, 'Then they cry unto the Lord in their trouble and he saveth them out of their distresses', and who has already suffered

VIII *The Falling Angel, 1923-33-47*

through his prophesied martyrdom all the agonies and humiliations ever destined for man. That the painter was moved by the idea of Jesus as a martyr is evident from another painting that shows the same Christlike figure – *Martyrdom* (1940).

This time the figure of the self-sacrificing martyr is bound to the stake. Instead of a halo he wears a Russian peasant's cap. In this picture, too, turmoil and destruction prevail. The street with the burning houses vanishes into the distance – a road of horrors without end. The ochre houses are streaked with dirt, the flames licking up from them thrust their vapours into masses of clouds as suffocating as tar fumes. The clear part of the sky, from which a cow and a cock come soaring down with a candlestick and a ladder, is a radiant turquoise blue and geranium red. Against the chained legs of the martyr leans a mourning female figure with a pink veil – a note of melancholy sweetness in contrast to the raging inferno in the background.

Both pictures are bold in composition and in the combination of realistic and abstract elements. But Chagall's 'realism', like the realism of Rembrandt, El Greco and Goya, is an expressive realism whose aim is not to imitate an object's visual appearance, but to portray its poetic force.

Chagall was painting the second picture when the Germans launched their attack on France and occupied Paris. These two works raised Chagall to the plane of the great accusers and passionate chroniclers among painters, at a time when he and his family were forced to the realization that they could not go on living under a Vichy Government. They were not destined to remain much longer in France. 'Le poète est chassé d'exil en exil et n'aura jamais demeure assurée', wrote Maurice de Guérin a century before. Chagall's approaching homelessness was likewise the fatal consequence of a human and artistic destiny.

In 1939 Chagall and his wife had moved to Gordes, near Marseilles. When the war broke out in September, Chagall at first continued to work unfalteringly. As late as February 1940 he even went to Paris, where the Galerie Mai was showing an exhibition of his latest works. He stayed there until shortly before the occupation of the city by German troops. From this moment on he and his family were no longer safe under the Vichy Government, and he had to stake everything on leaving France. An invitation from the director of the Museum of Modern Art in New York helped him to obtain an exit permit for himself and his pictures. But another year elapsed before the Chagall family were able to set foot on American soil. The pictures that had been sent by goods train to Lisbon went astray and wandered for months around Spain. 'Here in the harbour', wrote Chagall to an American friend, 'close to the ship, I discovered hundreds of my Jews with bag and baggage. I have never experienced such a sad event as when an author and his heroes take the same ship...'

The uprooting from French soil, the uncertain fate that awaited Chagall and millions of his race, the reports of the concentration camps and the atrocities committed against the Jews, had a profoundly depressing effect on him. This depression persisted after his arrival in New York, where he first lived. There were friends, certainly, and he derived some consolation from being able once more to stand at his easel and work; but his frame of mind was communicated to the pictures he now painted.

He produced wintry landscapes containing variations on the melancholy notes that rang out in his earlier paintings *Solitude* and *The Violinist in the Snow.* Along the snow-covered street of Vitebsk rides a *Harlequin Family* on a horse. The clown in his checked costume, the madonna-like figure of the woman with the child in her arms, the yellow flickering candle in the snow, and the dark raven under the bowed head of the horse are spellbound into the semblance of a still life within the enclosing triangle of the brightly lit street that tapers away to the upper edge of the picture. The dark, abandoned houses that form the frame emphasize the feeling of sadness and loneliness.

In the painting *In the Night* (1943) a pair of embracing lovers know one another full of tender terror; the bride's veil becomes one with the white of the nocturnal snow, which is illumined by the sickle of the moon and the light of a lamp that sinks down from the sky.

In the gouache *The Sleigh*, of the same year, a peasant sledge with horns speeds through an autumn night whose landscape shines pale green, yellow and lilac in the light that falls upon it from the horizon. The ragged branches of the leafless trees beside a distant farmstead tower in the reflection of a mystically shimmering crescent moon. The sleigh is simultaneously the body of an over life-size, lilac-coloured and likewise horned woman's head with a wide-open eye and a mouth that is lascivious with movement. The vehicle is driven by a small peasant figure in pale red squatting on the antlers of the sleigh cracking a whip. A picture of visionary power – its various parts hurtle along like phantoms from archaic states of consciousness. Looking at this scene one is reminded of Baudelaire's saying: 'La grande poésie est essentiellement bête, elle croit et c'est ce qui fait sa gloire et sa force.'

War (1943) is a direct expression of the frightfulness of contemporary events: on the same wintry street horses rear with horror, carts and sleighs break in pieces, the face of a madonna sailing through the firelit sky, whose hair also licks out like tongues of flame, and of a man with a pack on his back who is falling sideways beneath the hooves of a leaping horse – we have met this man before – attest the horror of the hour. Fire glows from the snow-covered roofs of the houses, through the billowing clouds of smoke a horde of soldiery advances with fixed bayonets. In the street a dead man lies with outstretched limbs. Were not the terrors and torments of this picture foreshadowed in the painting *Candles in a Dark Street* of 1908? This example once again discloses the logic in the evolution of Chagall's pictorial ideas, a logic drawn from quite special realms of thinking and feeling.
Another painting of 1943 is *The Yellow Crucifixion,* which has a colour scheme unusual for Chagall: an agitated metallic yellow, orange and patchy brown – dark and earthy – in the lower part; glowing red in the middle; and luminous lilac shadows at the top. Christ on the cross, with head erect, like a yellowed ivory statue, with the modelling almost of an old master and reminiscent of El Greco in the elongated body; a wide open green Torah scroll from which all the print has been expunged save the name 'Vitebsk'; below this a soaring angel, also in green and brownish yellow, and a madonna on a purple animal, a female figure with naked bosom shimmering gold and a blue face lit by an inner fire. In front of this trinity of ikon-like severity, the elements of the picture form a triangle whose apex reaches down to the lower edge; the background dissolves into individual scenes whose naively dramatic quality recalls peasant votive images. There are the lamenting Jews, the man with a ladder ... In the dirty brown waves of a stretch of water that spills over on to the street and reaches to the horizon, swimming women wail and a ship is sinking. This work radiates the mystery of an altar picture belonging to some alien culture, before whose power we shudder, of whose meaning we have an inkling without understanding the language in which it addresses us ... We feel the tensions of the symbolic

references which in this work – more than ever before – have been completely fused with the form and colour.

In a painter like Chagall the development from a depressively restrained chromatic scale to the exciting colour schemes of the last picture did not take place without cause: as so often in the career of this painter, the starting-point and stages in his artistic evolution are marked by events in his life.

In spring 1942 the famous choreographer Leonide Massine, who was the director of a ballet company in Mexico, asked Chagall to design the costumes and décor for the ballet *Aleko*, and to supervise their execution. Chagall accepted this commission with delight; he moved to Mexico City with his family, and set to work. The plot of the ballet is taken from Pushkin's poem *The Gypsies*. Aleko is the hero of a tragic love-story. Tired of his normal surroundings, he leaves the haunts of civilization and joins a band of gypsies. He loves the beautiful daughter of the grey-haired chief, but she betrays him with a young gypsy, whereupon Aleko kills both of them and is then cast out by the gypsies.

This romantic ballad of the steppes, to which Tchaikovsky lent equally passionate and elegiac tone-colours, appeared to Chagall at this point in his exile like a dream from a more poetic world. He lavished the wealth of his pictorial metaphor on four huge background decorations. The purple cock of passion storms through the blue night, lovers sail along beneath the rays of the moon, the glow of the sun is drowned in the maize-yellow and blue of a riparian-landscape..., above the roofs of a dream city a prancing white horse leaps across a background of glowing red.

Chagall's sojourn in Mexico also restored to him for several months the glow of a southern sun and revealed to him a splendour of colour such as he had never known before. The life of the Mexican peon, with its outer frugality and inner joyousness, its unreflecting thought and action, reminded him of the people in his Russian homeland. Only in Mexico the colour contrasts were more violent, the sun harsher, the nights more luminous. Chagall painted a number of gouaches. A characteristic picture of this period is *The Sleeping Guitar* (1943).

The background is a velvety moss-green with patina-brown, cloudy shadows, filled by the vast curve of a hill that rises to the upper edge of the picture against a sky of cobalt and violet. In this drunken blue of night float a milk-white moon and pallid stars. On the curve of the hill's disk that symbolizes the globe, a crouching peon in a pointed hat clings with mingled curiosity and fear. The contours of his body are silhouetted with white and dark lines drawn in the blue and purple of the sky. The guitar slips from his hand, his eyes in the circle of his face gaze in astonishment at the idyll in the foreground: there is the Chagallian 'animal', this time with two heads, one of them greenish-white with great turquoise-blue eyes, the other orange in colour, raised into the air and wildly gnashing its teeth; over the second head gleam the letters M E X I C O. On the animal, half sitting and half floating, rides a female figure in a skirt and blouse; the colours are like enamel flux – bright blue and brownish red. On her back she carries a child. To the left of the woman the picture is closed by a bouquet of flowers dabbed in with touches of lemon yellow, geranium-red and lilac. Between the animal's heads and the peon, sketched into the brown shadows of the hill, is a ghostly, bear-like monster. There is something wild and ecstatic about the picture; it has a touch of the burlesque and humorous, such as we see in many of Joan Miró's creations.

The same forcefulness characterizes *The Juggler* (1943), of which, like many of Chagall's works, there are two versions – in this case a gouache and an oil painting.

In the gouache, the colours green, blue, yellow, vermilion and violet flow together to form shapes in which the attributes of Chagall's imagery unite in the figure of a man-bird-angel that fills the whole area of the picture. The head is a cock's, the comb forms the neck, the hands are at the same time claws, the body gleams with the green of meadows above which a sun is glowing. Interwoven with the light is the figure of a woman playing the violin. The sun might be the breast of a hermaphroditic being, the foot of the violin-playing woman enters the body of the harlequin-monster, the sex, loins and thighs shimmer cobalt, and red flashes dart through their luminous blue – the veins; moons and suns revolve... The arena is swirling fleshy purple in which swims a goat's head that might have been painted by Soutine. The concentric rings of the seats revolve with the ghostly contours of the spectators. Over everything the moon soars triumphant yet not without emitting kindly and gentle rays, and the juggler sails along with huge white wings and a clock folded like a cloth over his outstretched arm, a clock such as Dali has painted but possessed here of a totally different meaning.

This painting shows Chagall in all his old power, as a 'beast of art', as an American critic called him, as 'l'orage enchanté', as Raissa Maritain has described him. Here he is close to the Surrealists, and yet this work eludes Surrealist criteria. For all the violence of its forms and colours, we find in them that innocence which so often goes hand in hand with the incomprehensible and barbaric – and not only in the dreams and actions of children. This picture rends *and* atones; behind the demon's mask we glimpse the grace of future redemption. Finally, the picture mirrors its creator's fears, despair and horror no less than the triumph of creativeness over the terrors of this earth.

'In the Shell of his Universe'

We have already spoken of the nature of 'space' in Chagall's pictorial world, of its affinity with space as it appears to the child and the dreamer. As Chagall's picture developed an ever- increasing poetic density his conception of pictorial space also grew deeper. What a difference there is between the cubistically interlocking components of many of his early paintings and the increasingly organic fusion of the 'inner worlds' in his later works. Standing before them one has the feeling that the painter has in each case created a new centre of pictorial space into which he retires as though into a cave, apparently in retreat from the world, but in reality impelled solely by the urge to approach the very core of the world's mystery.

Aldous Huxley, speaking in his *Meditations on El Greco* of the picture portraying the dream of Philip II, in which a gigantic whale's gullet swallows up the outcasts of this world, points out that El Greco's visions resemble those that appeared to Jonah in the belly of the whale. Thus the Cretan painter's pictorial spaces, with their concave, contracting backgrounds, their structures that resemble disintegrating flesh, and their 'entrail-like' drapery, are a concrete depiction of what Jonah experienced in the immense living and pulsating cavern of Leviathan.

New possibilities of apprehension and interpretation of periods of art, of styles, of individual works of art and their creators present themselves if, utilizing this new insight, we grasp the identity between the space portrayed in a picture and the space within the artist's own heart, if we regard the spatial element in a painting as a negative shape, a matrix within which we can recognize the dimensions, the structure and the physiognomy of the creative soul. Within this matrix the shores, the mountains, the expanses of sky spread out, the universe contracts into rooms, grottoes and shells that are filled with the silence, the whispering, the breathing of their inhabitants. Within this matrix we find the dream vistas of Klee's paintings, the solitudes in the works of Picasso, and Chagall's visionary world wrapped closely around their dreamlike inhabitants . . .

Space in Chagall's pictures is the product of the interaction of three realms. First, the realm of colours and shapes whose origin seems to lie beyond the surface of the canvas; second, the realm formed by the symbols and beings operating on this surface; and third, the realm contributed by those figures which, because of the suggestive power of their formal and dramatic values seem to be soaring *in front of* the picture plane. In this way a kind of vaulted pictorial space, a hemispherical shell, is created which opens towards the spectator, growing towards him from the edges and including him as a participant in the events within this space. In order to enhance this effect, Chagall often enlarges the elements near the edges of his paintings – particularly those in the upper section – beyond their normal proportions and so makes them figures in a new foreground. These figures – acrobats under the dome of the circus tent, lovers in the vault of the night, in a nest of leaves and flowers – float in the resultant vaulted space.

How are we to interpret this phenomenon? Psychoanalytically, perhaps, as Freud interpreted the cave motif in Leonardo's famous painting? Or should we see this liking for enclosed spaces, as Huxley does in the case of El Greco's picture, as a sign of the painter's inability to pass out of his environment into the infinite? Is it not enough to confine ourselves to noting that this phenomenon is the outcome of many different operations and aims arising out of the

IX *The Sleigh, 1943*

creative process itself? We shall, however, be justified in enquiring what possibilities of artistic revelation are gained by this particular form of pictorial construction. The principal gain is the effect of suggestion. The fact that the spectator is looking at events compressed into a closed space brings the components of the picture closer to him. He finds himself touched by their breath, lit up by their reflected glow, caught in the spell of their glances and gestures. For a spellbound moment the outer world fades away, the spectator becomes one with the picture. That Chagall himself felt similarly as he was conceiving many of his paintings is proved by the aims he had in view when he produced the murals and stage sets in the New Jewish Theatre...

That Chagall consciously or unconsciously aimed at achieving this 'inner space' is made evident by a comparison between *The Lovers in the Lilacs* and the paintings of the years 1943 to 1947. In *The Lovers in the Lilacs* we can still observe his efforts to create a symbol of enclosedness inside the painting as a whole. In the pictures of the latter years, however, the whole painted surface becomes the living wall of a shell. There is the red of the flaming sky in which soar the heavy body of an animal whose two faces are those of a pair of lovers, an upside down birch tree with green twigs, the outline of a huge cock, and the crescent moon – *Listening to the Cock* (1943). Violet shadows form the walls of a cloud-cavern through which flies the lilac-coloured figure of a bride – *Violet Filigree* (1945). In *The City Falls Asleep* (1945) the fantastically metamorphosed pair on a trapeze – this time the dancer wears an iridescent blue-green garment while an emerald green horse's head sprouts from her shoulders – are enclosed by glowing flames. The bridal veil of the beloved in the blue-green nocturnal undergrowth of *The Siren's Tail* (1945) shimmers like the raiment of a naiad and yet is full of maidenly modesty. This painting recalls Christian Morgenstern's saying that 'we all live at the bottom of the sea – the sea of air'.

In the painting *Autour d'elle* (1945), which now hangs in the Musée d'Art Moderne and represents a more intimate version of the picture *A ma femme* painted a little earlier, there emerges from the sacral blue of the background – which is filled by the painter at his easel, an angel, a bird carrying a candle and a bridal pair – another spatial dimension: moonlit Vitebsk enclosed in a sphere. Here one shell is contained inside another, a kernel in the fruit-pulp of a more comprehensive world, a glimmering planet in the cosmos of dreams.

In the latter picture we find no trace of the harsh brilliance of the Mexico paintings. This is the old Chagallian world, deepened and transfigured by a new sort of devoutness in the pictorial style, by a mystic rapture. What was it that conjured this note into being?

After their return from Mexico, Chagall and Bella lived at High Fall in the Catskill Mountains, a town on the mountainous northern border of New York State. A photograph taken in the early summer of 1944 shows Chagall and Bella on the shores of Cranberry Lake, sitting among great boulders and tree trunks and branches bleached by time and weather. Chagall is using one of these branches as an easel, another supports a finished work – the gouache with the racing sleigh-head. Chagall is gazing at Bella, who is holding his palette and looking at the work in process. They are both smiling – but this gaiety is more than a pose for the photographer. 'Et la peinture n'est plus rien d'autre qu'une façon d'aimer . . .', Chagall once said.

In September of the same year Bella died from a virus infection.

The pictures of the ensuing years are once more invocations of lover's happiness, born of the memory of the wife he had lost.
The night through which a clinging couple glide in *The Bare Cloud* (1945) is ashy grey. In the background stand the motionless houses of Vitebsk. A lamenting female figure in blue, her hair falling down over her shoulders, squats in front of a flowering tree. The moon drifts through the sunset sky. The bodies of the lovers are one with the yellow cloud that serves them as a bed. This incorporeal colour underlines the transfigured, otherworldly nature of their existence. Their demeanour expresses a deep fervour, such as can be born only of the shyness of first love or the wisdom that comes when the passions of this world have been left behind.
Beside the cloud-bed on which the two lovers are reclining emerges the shadow of a second bed. A cow crouches upon it accompanied by a violin and a bow. Flowers and leaves grow round the edges of the picture, and the border of a curtain may be seen drawn aside by the soaring figure of a youth.
The Spirit of the Town (1945) and *Self-Portrait with Clock* (1946) take up the Christ theme again. In the first picture, the main tone of which is a murky grey-blue, the sky, streets and houses are seen as though through a veil, the double-headed figure of the painter floats in front of the picture of the crucifixion pointing with passionately outstretched arm to the figure of Christ. The painter's second, green-shadowed face is gazing at the woman's figure hurtling down like a white flame beside him. Only a few colours glow out from the sombre background – a red tabernacle curtain, two blue animal figures, the violet clothing of the painter, and the figure of a girl holding a cock in the lower foreground.
In the second picture the artist is once more in front of a painting of Christ that rests on an easel. But the character of this scene is more lyrical, more restrained.

In the picture of the crucifixion a bridal figure approaches the face of the Redeemer – the painter's head is bowed before these events, and the head of an animal that has grown out of his shoulder bows in worship with him. Above them the old pendulum clock flies through the background of flickering space; instead of wings the clock has been given arms and hands, with which it blesses the encounters of this hour.

'Ringing Forms, Filled with Passion'

Closely as the events in Chagall's life and his artistic creations mutually determine one another, there is no precise historical continuity in his themes, no clearly perceptible succession of cause and effect such as biographers are accustomed to search for so keenly. We have already noted that Chagall wants nothing to do with 'themes' in the literary, anecdotal sense. He thinks, as he has repeatedly stressed, in terms of pictorial construction, of the distribution and arrangement of certain colours on a flat plane. 'I strive primarily', he once said, 'to build up my picture architectonically, just as the Impressionists and the Cubists used to do in their day. The Impressionists covered their canvas with light and dark patches of colour, the Cubists with square, triangular, and round shapes. Instead of this, I try to fill my canvas with objects and figures which I employ in place of such shapes, with ringing forms filled with passion that are to create an additional dimension such as cannot be attained with the pure geometry of Cubist lines or Impressionist dabs of colour.'

He is suspicious of words like 'fairy tale', 'fantasy' and 'symbolism'. 'Our whole inner world is reality, perhaps more so than the visible world. If we describe everything that appears to us illogical as "fantastic", a "fairy tale" or a "figment of the imagination", we are admitting that we do not understand nature.'
On being asked about the continual recurrence of certain motifs and figures in his pictures, he replied: 'That I have made the cows, girls, cocks and houses of provincial Russia my fundamental forms is explained by the fact that they belong to the milieu from which I originated and they have undoubtedly left the deepest imprint on my visual memory. However vitally and variously a painter may react to the atmosphere and influences of his later surroundings, a certain "aroma" of his birthplace will always remain attached to his work... Thus I hope I have preserved the influences of my childhood in more than merely their material aspect.'
From this point of view, Chagall is right when he considers himself a painter who 'is more abstract than Mondrian and Kandinsky'. By 'abstract' he under-

stands everything which 'becomes spontaneously both plastically and psychically living through a scale of contrasts, and fills both the picture and the eye of the beholder with representations of new and strange elements'.

The unprejudiced spectator of Chagall's works will also respond to the themes, the subject matter of these pictures – and all the more so because the themes comply with the demands of a work of art, that is to say, because they have become 'plastic' components of the painting. Chagall's poet friends, who often wrote about his works, were particularly concerned with these figures and symbols. Similarly, I have given special attention to the reality which they represent, meaning by 'reality' always that inner reality of which Chagall himself speaks. Above and beyond Chagall's own explanations, the spectator must be free to occupy himself with those manifestations in the painter's work which appeal particularly to the antennae of his inner perception – the lovers, the circus performers and harlequins, the animals and the figures of Christ.

Chagall also acknowledges the justice of this way of looking at his work: 'The painter should never interpose his person between his work and the spectator. A third person may well attempt to interpret an artist's work without doing it any harm . . .'

We have seen how Chagall takes up again symbols which he has used before, changing, animating and enriching them. Having given them a new body, a fresh expressive value, he turns to others, until one day he picks up the old symbols once more, coming back to them as to an artistic and human task whose ultimate solution is unforseeable. Thus he unhesitatingly creates various groups of pictures at one and the same time; and yet there does arise something in the nature of a sequence, the rhythm of which corresponds to the rhythm of his own eventful life.

The Fire Bird

Only a short while after Bella's death Chagall received a commission to design and supervise sets and costumes for a performance by the Ballet Theatre in New York of Stravinsky's *Fire Bird*. This work gave him an opportunity to translate his grief for Bella into a medium that was at once a testimony and a consolation.

Chagall's stage designs – even his earlier ones – never occupy a place apart from the rest of his work: their themes and their artistic and formal problems are a continuation of those of his paintings. Moreover, the fact that this ballet is based on an old Russian fairy tale enabled him to utilize many of his favourite pictorial motifs in his designs.

A prince is hunting a fire bird, which buys freedom from his pursuer with a golden feather. At a magic word, this feather calls up the saving presence of the almighty bird. When the prince and twelve virgins find themselves in the power of sorcerers, fiends and demons in a burning forest, the feather shows its miraculous power. The prince invokes the fire bird, which destroys the evil powers and aids him to lead home the bewitched princesses.

Chagall created a curtain and three settings. The first setting is a magic forest depicted with an infinite wealth of visual forms. At one point the forest is seen from in front, at another from above, while one stretch of forest stands on its head, so that the upper and lower halves of the picture appear like each other's reflection in a mirror. It is as though the forest were seen from all the changing viewpoints of the bird that flies to and fro in its midst.

The second setting shows the magician's castle, built on the enormous body of a dragonlike winged monster. The third portrays the wedding feast: a universe of ringing blues in the midst of which circle red planets. A pair of lovers are soaring towards the largest of these planets; the bride's dress flashes down to the earth like the tail of a meteor.

On the curtain Chagall's cavernlike interior world yawns once more, and through it sweeps the red-glowing bird on its mighty pinions. It has two heads, one crowned and triumphant, one the jubilant head of a woman. The bodies of the bird and the woman are one, and yet the former lends its enigmatic quality to the latter, thereby transferring it on to a strange and mystic plane. The female figure stretches her arms out blissfully in front of her, blossoms fall from her hands like snow, and the wings of the bird are spread above her, royally protective. In an onrush of every shade of purple the bird-woman-monster, terrible and charming at the same time, swoops over the flaming valley with its frightened houses, its tiny inhabitants and creatures. It engenders its light from within itself; the blaze on the horizon is only the reflection of its wings, before which even the crescent moon turns black.

Chagall transposed the theme of the fiery bird and flaming landscapes into other works painted in these years – for example, a gouache of 1945, which is filled by an enormous red cock through whose garment of flames the figure of a bride soars up towards the disc of the moon. This painting is called *Flames Become Hot and Red.* Finally, we must also reckon among these paintings the monumental *Falling Angel,* finished in 1947, which we have already discussed and which elevates the same theme to an apocalyptic level.

The last pictures Chagall painted in America before returning to France were oil paintings and gouaches for lithographs, in which his painful and joyful experiences were fused and expressed in works of art of unique beauty. *Nocturne* (1947) is the title of an oil painting in rich hues on a background of sea-green and coral red. Through the night sky rent by lightning fly a snow-white bride of the wind and a ruby-red horse. A candlestick pours out the liquid gold of its light. From the bottom of the picture rise a glimmering purple village, a flashing metallic-blue church spire, and a huge foaming copper-red flowering tree. The sickle of the moon in the black shadows of the sky, and the flaming outline of a cock in the extreme foreground, allow us to glimpse the distance of a spatial dimension which here again is not measureable reality, but the expanse of a metaphysical world. Poets with an Orphic sense of the universe – Georg Trakl, Rimbaud and Francis Thompson, for example – have recorded similar apocalyptic visions in the music of their words.

The thirteen lithographs for *The Arabian Nights,* which Chagall made for Pantheon Books, New York, are likewise to be regarded, print by print, as manifestations of the same poetic world, as independent works of art. The figures of lovers, princesses and dancing girls are wedded to the symbols of the sun, moon and stars, of clouds and waves and Chagallian animals to create a world of delight, of amorous seduction and complaint. And yet here, once more, nothing is illustrative or anecdotal, all the beauty and magic of the stories are transposed into a very carefully thought out and subtle arrangement of colours, patches and lines. In harmony with the delicate character of the designs, pastel shades preponderate. But Chagall's delicacy is never that of the painted porcelain medallion – it is fierce and innocent, barbaric and refined. In this respect – that is to say, in their poetic essence – these lithographs, which bear the typical imprint of Chagall, have a close inner affinity with the Arabian stories they illustrate.

The last works Chagall produced in America seem partially to anticipate an art of the future about which he spoke during a conference of teachers and students of Mount Holyoke-College in summer 1943. The subject of his lecture was 'Impressions of French Painting', and he made it the occasion for an exposition of his own experiences and artistic aims. At the end he cried out:

'... Mankind is looking for something new. It is looking for its own original power of expression, like that of the primitives, of the people who opened their mouths for the first time to utter their unique truth ... I do not know – who can see into the future? – what outer and inner shape the French art of the future will assume. Will there be a continuous renewal of its former marvellous vision and cult of form? Will its former vision be replaced by a new inner vision, by an entirely new way of looking at the world ...?'

Was Chagall aware of the extent to which he had already realized some part of these visions of the future in his latest works?

In spring 1947 Chagall returned to France. The great retrospective exhibition held the same year in the Musée d'Art Moderne, Paris, established him in his true artistic rank. His work was thoroughly modern in all its phases, and equal in originality and inventiveness to that of his youngest contemporaries. It seemed to anticipate a great many trends that had won general recognition only as a result of the most recent developments in painting. The consistency with which Chagall had followed his chosen path became manifest. He had put into effect the prophecy which his poet friend Canudo had made almost in jest three decades before: he had become the greatest colourist of his day. The exhibition was also shown in London and Amsterdam. The example which these works gave to a world suffering from the after-effects of a murderous war created an artistic and moral sensation.

Chagall lived first at Orgeval, near Paris. Then he moved south, to the Riviera. He stayed for three months at St Jean Cap-Ferrat, once more tirelessly creating. *St Jean Cap-Ferrat* is the title of a painting (1949) that became a song of praise to the imperishable delight of love and the beauty of the Côte d'Azur. In this picture a young couple lean into the blue of a moonlit night filled with the perfume of summer fruits and flowers and the shimmer of the sea.

In 1949 Chagall moved to Vence, where he went to live in the villa called *Les Collines* situated in a romantic park at the foot of the Baous Mountains. Attached to the house is a studio formerly occupied by Paul Valéry. This move brought Chagall close in a spatial sense also to two other masters among modern painters: Matisse, who likewise lived at Vence, and Picasso, who was producing his ceramics at Vallauris.

One of the first pictures he painted at Vence is called *The Red Sun* (1949). It now hangs in the entrance hall of Chagall's house, and the glow of its colours emerging from the darkness greets all who enter. An elongated female figure in an intensely blue dress soars diagonally across the background, her face, neck and naked breasts modelled with patina-green shadows. Flying to meet her comes the figure of a youth in luminous yellow that cuts across the splintered red of a sun. The picture is dominated by red, yellow and blue, the primal triad of the colours, the spectrum of the sun. The spaces between are filled by figures, animals and flowers in gentler hues that soften the imperious major note of the three primaries. The outlines of the figures are emphatic and forceful, resembling the network of lead in stained-glass windows between which the light streams in all its brilliance. If we compare this picture with those of earlier 'soaring couples' – here, too, white lines are stretched across the surface, the

x *The Banks of the Seine, 1953*

ropes of imaginary trapezes – we feel how the paint increasingly asserts its own life and identity, how a mode of pictorial expression is created that has little to do with what has now become for Chagall a conventional theme. The subject matter here is the paint itself, it radiates in pure joy against the background of the night, its eternal counterpart.

It is easy to understand that Chagall, in evolving his conception of painting, should have sought a 'motif' on a par with the expressive power of his colours. Biblical themes were in the forefront of his mind, because he had resumed work on the etchings for the Old Testament. Thus one of his pictures of this period – a painting as large as a mural – bears the title *King David* (1950/51).

The dominant figure of the King in his embroidered purple robe is placed to one side; this enlarges the main expanse of the picture with its varied backgrounds and scenes. Bands of intense colours grow, curve and lean towards the purple – a turquoise, a vermilion, a violet, the bright yellow and the white meteor's tail of a female figure sailing upright through the air. In the depths of the picture suns circle triumphantly above the pinnacles of Jerusalem, while circles of light stud the surface like planets. Spirals and rays of light dart through the spaces of the picture, split up and add new dimensions to its activity. Every element seems to have been introduced in order to intensify every other: here the colours glow in their abstract, dynamic relationships, there the lines and forms of the composition divide, intersect, support and combat one another in a rhythm that forces everything into a coherent whole. These abstract, plastic components are in turn bound to real and conceivable phenomena which, at the same time, possess a legendary, mythical character: the figure of the King with crown and harp, the green rabbi bowing humbly in the centre of the picture, the bridal pair paying homage to one another, the painter with the faithful making their way in procession from the Holy City. Alongside the clearly distinct and separate major colours, more lyrical chromatic passages stand out. All these components are drawn into relation by a subtle intelligence that fits the divergent parts into a rich whole.

Two further paintings that are also on the scale of murals blaze out like mighty ikons. The themes of these works, *Moses* (1950/52) and *The Crossing of the Red Sea* (1954/55), were likewise prefigured in the etchings for the Bible. In these, too, we can see Chagall's endeavour to enrich his means of expression, to create images of enhanced power and significance. In these paintings we see all his earlier *dramatis personae* united as though in apotheosis.

Perhaps it was the inner and outer magnitude of works such as these that suggested to Chagall's friends at Vence the idea of creating for them a building, a kind of worldly shrine, where people could receive their message in undisturbed tranquillity. The pictures demand to be looked at in a room consecrated by

the spectator's reverence; in this way they fulfil a function that passes beyond the purely artistic and aesthetic sphere.
The last-named painting was finished at the beginning of 1955. It was the highlight of the first large-scale German exhibition of Chagall's work held in Hanover in May of the same year. The organizers of this exhibition had brought the painting still wet from the wall of Chagall's studio.
It has already been pointed out that no strict chronological sequence can be established in Chagall's work, because the painter – in conformity with the richness of his artistic nature – often interrupted the execution of even his major works to resume thematic cycles he had begun long before. Here we are concerned with the 'Paris' sequence which Chagall painted in the years 1952 to 1955.

Thanks to Paris

Three times Chagall came into contact with the city of Paris: three times he embodied his impressions of this city in a cycle of paintings. First it was the Eiffel Tower, the exciting, inspiring, threatening emblem of the other, the western world, to which he opposed his memories of Vitebsk. The force of his childhood myths came up against the mighty symbol of a spirit bent upon reaching the source of poetic impulses.
On the second occasion Paris seemed to Chagall, after the breakdown of the old Russian world and the mortification he had suffered from a regime that was hostile to art, like an island of light, beauty and liberty. He celebrated the enchantments of this city, and the people who moved about in it, in paintings of great beauty. Vitebsk became a dream which, because it was dreamed in happiness, was transfigured by the lustre of his present surroundings.
The third meeting followed Chagall's return from an agonizing exile. 'When I came back to France after years in America, the romantic appearance of Paris, still vivid, still luminous after the terrible years through which the world had passed, made a deep impression on me', he comments. He gave artistic expression to this meeting from the south of France, from his rose-wreathed studio at Vence. The result was the sequence of pictures bearing the title *Thanks to Paris* – twenty-nine paintings exhibited by the Galerie Maeght at Paris in June 1954.
Like Vitebsk years before, Paris had now become a dream. Like every dream that evokes the past, these pictures – for all their beauty – are permeated by that melancholy which always accompanies recollection.
The 'subject' of each of these paintings is some landmark of the metropolis, from which the picture takes its name – the Opéra, the Champ-de-Mars, the Eiffel Tower, St-Germain-des-Prés... But these 'subjects' have no other purpose than

to make the poetic thrill of actuality inescapably manifest through the medium of a recognizable piece of reality. They prove to be examples of that 'individual presence' from which, according to Goethe, 'the deeper meaning of the universal grows'. Chagall's paintings of Paris are entirely different from those of Utrillo or the Impressionists, which despite all their poetic abstraction, remain in the best sense of the word 'views'. Chagall's pictures represent primarily his dreams, his love for man and beast. 'Even when I looked at Paris, I saw nothing but myself', he had stated decades before.

In one painting the sky glows orange-yellow, the silhouette of the city with the Eiffel Tower, the Cathedral and the Pont-Neuf shimmers white and mauve. The streets, avenues and quays, along which lovers roam, are bordered with pink blossoms. The tip of the Eiffel Tower splits in pieces in the vermilion beam of its upside-down shadow. A flaming bow of red and yellow circles arches over the bridge. One sun gives birth to another, larger one. Through the brightness of the firmament sail the lightly sketched faces of a couple united in an embrace. A hint of Vitebsk appears in a grey, white and pink silhouette whose chromatic scale is lower than that of the dominant background.

The double face of the lovers glimmers opal and slate-grey against the black disc of an enormous moon in another picture, painted lengthways, with a moss-green sky shot through by a multitude of forms, shapes and bodies, and a section of the city with its houses, its bridge and the river emerging cobalt blue from the shadows of the night. Brief touches of complementary colours are set in the juxtaposed blue and green – a brick red and a restrained cobalt, in the shapes of plants and animals. In the left-hand lower corner emerald green, lemon yellow, coral red and white gleam with a festive radiance in the outlines of a flowering tree.

In the third painting a mother and child, a transparent cerulean blue and deep purple, are soaring above the Quai des Fleurs. The basic colour of the shadows that envelop the picture is an even more intense blue. Here the real subject of the painting is the blue colour that deepens into a cavern of the universe.

In the next painting of this sequence the blue sky arches above the tower of Notre-Dame cathedral. The remaining shapes in the picture – the silhouette of Montmartre with the glittering church of Sacré-Cœur – are all pushed to the edge and serve the sole purpose of rendering the life of this blue more clearly manifest. The Gothic gargoyle is accompanied by the Chagallian cock, and thereby loses all its devilish appearance, becoming an entirely radiant and kindly creature.

Before every one of these paintings we witness how objects that remind us of reality slip away from us, how their place is taken by mysteries that were hiding behind the objects, mysteries that have now become colour, planes and shapes of colour. Chagall's remark that he considers himself more abstract than the so-called 'abstract painters' holds good for these pictures too. How far Chagall advances beyond the given theme to ultimate artistic and moral truth is shown by two striking examples.

In the first, *The Seine Bridges* (1954), the main artery of Paris once more shimmers across the picture, as though seen by someone soaring above it. The ribbon of the Seine, the bridges, church towers and countless roofs appear oxidized to a patina green, in the midst of which certain spots flash out like patches of bright metal on a relief that has just been cleaned. A purple madonna with phosphorescent contours soars along upright, shading with her violet wings the city and river and the half lying, half floating naked couple in cobalt blue inside the cave of the lower half of the picture. The outlines of their soft, slender limbs are as though carved of moonstone, the depths shimmer with mysteries known only to the lovers in the magical conjunction of this hour. The Chagallian animal, a cow-like figure, crouches on the cloudy edge of the cavern, a symbol of the peace of this nocturnal myth.

The largest of the paintings, *The Roofs*, is divided into three diagonal bands of colour – black, red and white – that surge up from lower left to upper right. The outline of the banks of the Seine emerges from the upper ink-black band; out of the central band of red, split up into an abundance of prismatic planes, grows the street of Vitebsk with its houses, rooms and alleyways. Everything is tangible and yet transparent, like the walls in a dream that reveal rather than conceal the depths behind them. The rooms are full of figures we know from Chagall's earliest paintings. Above these thousand-facetted planes a red youth bends shyly down, a palette in his hand. His body forms a curve that takes the edge off the prismatic angularity of the compacted cubes. The arc of this figure is counterbalanced by a huge sun in soft yellow that envelops a pink courtyard. Into this sun grows the figure of a violet student carrying a Torah scroll. The double figure of the lovers emerges from the right-hand lower corner. A farm-cart goes spanking along the street, the driver brandishing his whip – a tiny speck of impotent haste in the silence of this song of praise, in the midst of which, against the background of a Russian church, shines the figure of the Crucified.

Once before, the Southern French landscape has astonished Chagall with its wealth of colours and its lyrical atmosphere, had captivated him with the beauty of its flowers and foliage. These impressions found their way into his paintings of that period, refined their *peinture* and lent them a hitherto unknown radiance. At the same time, their colours and forms became more organic, more 'natural'. Chagall had never worked 'from nature', but he had always striven to create 'like nature'.

If, during the twenties, the study of colour in nature had helped him to discover and cultivate the 'chemistry' of colours, he now awoke to the essence of nature, to the force at work within it that finds expression in 'matter' as he understands the word. Chagall wished the colours and forms of his paintings to sing like 'matter', the lines in his drawings to possess the same tremulous life as the contours of objects, the dots and patches to vibrate and dance.

Nature and 'matter' as Chagall found them at Vence appeared, for all their southern ripeness and sweetness, to be stubborn, full of independent life, tangible and yet laden with mystery. Natural form and structure proves as delicate as filigree, transparent as air, soft as fruit pulp, pliant and firm as leaf and earth, rough and intractable as the boughs, bark and rock. In addition, seen with Chagall's eyes, they testified to the loving kindness of their creator. The drawings and paintings, the ceramics and sculptures, which Chagall produced at Vence were testimonies to his confrontation with nature, a confrontation that led him not to strive and compete with nature, but to become one with nature and glorify it.

One of the results was a profusion of Indian-ink drawings. Drawing for its own sake was an activity in which Chagall had previously never engaged. 'Only during the last two years', he wrote in 1950, 'have I begun to occupy myself with Indian-ink drawings. They seemed to me a step forward in the quest for light, not colour. For light contains every conceivable colour, just as colour contains the whole of light. Strange. Since my return from America these Indian-ink drawings have forced their way into my soul where they never had any place before... In this world threatened by bombs and atomic energy one has a particular longing to bind oneself to this earth and become one with it.'

Up to the present we have seen the special quality of Chagall's drawing in the sensibility of its stroke, which obeys the slightest movement of the creative impulse, without sacrificing vigour to mannerism or expressiveness and vitality to stylization. Chagall satisfied the demand for originality in all his drawings:

not one resembles another in its structure and technique, and yet every one of them bears the stamp of his individuality.

The line, the spot, and the white area they enclose, are rich in plastic values. The task of the line and the dabbed in spot is not only to outline a visualized form, but also to be form themselves, a form that gains life and truth from the shape they enclose. Chagall was always gifted with the ability to give plastic value and symbolic force to the line and the other components of a graphic work in a very direct fashion. It is as though his hand, as it guides the pencil or the brush, is at once a perceiving, conceiving, depicting and transmuting organ. The forms seem to have been drawn effortlessly, and yet they are the product of intensely hard work: with Chagall a successful drawing always means a selected drawing, chosen out of a large number of earlier works as having hit the mark.

Proof of his exertions in the field of Graphic art is to be found in the countless drawings that accompany his vast *œuvre* as a painter, and also in the great graphic cycles. In addition to this, Chagall from the very beginning illustrated the books of verse and prose written by his friends, works by Soupault, Reverdy, Eluard, Coquiot, and many others. Later he made poignant pen-drawings for *Burning Lights*, the book of memoirs Bella wrote during their joint exile in the United States.

The drawings Chagall has made since moving to Vence show a growing tendency to develop into pictures. The accumulation and interpenetration of the component parts, and their poetic significance, achieve such a density that we cease to feel that we are looking at a drawing in the ordinary sense of the word. These Indian-ink drawings are mostly large. The subjects are crouching or lying nudes, lovers, still lifes and flowers in an almost Impressionist style, works that do not belie the spontaneous optical experience of the new environment. In these works, too, Chagall is not content merely to apprehend phenomena in the sense of *vite fait, vite vu;* what he puts down on paper is always translated into the realm of allegory.

Stimulated by the richness of the Provençal landscape, by the same life-affirming bucolic impulse, Dufy, Matisse and Picasso created similar songs of praise to the beauty of that which is. The urge to try their hand at ceramics and sculpture sprang from a need to draw close to the earth as embodied in the raw material of these arts. Had not Cézanne, confronted by the same landscape, already said that art was 'a harmony parallel with nature'?

We must welcome the fact that Chagall also employs these techniques and materials, and that in any exhibitions and collections which contain the graphic works of the great modern artists we also find those of Chagall. That this is more than a mere coincidence of art history, or the result of friendly competition between colleagues, is clear from the consistent and independent evolution through which Chagall's graphic art passed to reach this sensuous and psychic plenitude of expression.

Despite the differences in style and outlook, we are struck by the common element that runs through all his drawings, as though, guided by the same creative passion, the various routes all led to the same destination. In their ultimate density they are all striving towards the same core: the marrow of poetry and its aesthetic and moral truth. Such thoughts may enter the spectator's mind if he compares Chagall's drawings, lithographs and wash-drawings with Picasso's drawings of 1947, having as their theme *The Waking and the Sleeping*.

Naturally Vitebsk reappears and we meet the Eiffel Tower. One drawing testifies to the wisdom and profundity to which Chagall's graphic art has attained. The Eiffel Tower rises darkly in the shape of a mythical obelisk, the moon grows out of the firmament like a black planet, beneath which a pair of lovers soar, one flesh, one symbol, a monument to all passionate embraces.

Another drawing, *The Sturgeon* (1952), shows how the still-life quality of the subject can emerge through the timeless, spaceless ambit of a prophetic vision. The fish that fills the picture-surface horizontally is at once a shimmering, living and breathing animal, and a metaphor reduced to its ultimate form. A tentative horizon, a hint of reflections and waves on a lake, two birds flying overhead, the sketchy crescent of a boat, and the disc of a damply shimmering evening sun with its dark bridges of light on the water, transform the picture into a silent primeval landscape after which our humbled and disillusioned spirit yearns.

In spring 1950, the periodical *Verve* published in Paris by Tériade brought out a series of twenty-six facsimiles of Indian-ink drawings made by Chagall to illustrate Boccaccio's *Decameron*. These wash-drawings were contrasted with colour prints of medieval miniatures on the same theme.

In the postcard-sized parchment pictures the colourful and animated scenes of amorous seduction and jealousy were depicted with the same care, the same earnest attention to visible facts, as the pictures of the saints in religious manuscripts of the same period. As though on a stage, whose emerald green curtain is meticulously drawn back, we see a monk in a black habit embracing a Gothic beauty in a mauve dress on a scarlet cushion, while a fellow monk watches the couple through a key-hole. In another picture a nobleman clothed in costly blue, white and red stuffs lies beside his equally distinguished and coronetted wife on a green lawn enclosed by a neatly clipped hedge. Between the couple grows a birch-tree with heraldically spaced leaves and gleaming fruit. A jealous lover leans down from the tree-top.

XI *Red Nude, 1954-55*

Facing each of these medieval scenes – which Jacques Prévert calls in his introduction *'merveilleux vaudeville multicolore'* – is one of Chagall's 'illustrations', drawn with a reed pen and an ink wash and occupying the whole of a large page. Whereas the figures in the miniatures look like finely dressed puppets in a silent ballet, devoid of any emotion excited by atmosphere, passion or longing, Chagall's lovers are alive with the breath and vigour of fateful events. Nudes glimmer white against nocturnal backgrounds, floating like mythical beings between the earth and the moon; monuments to amorous union stand out darkly against a bright sky tinged by the rays of a black sun.
The medieval painter distinguished the figures of his comedies of love according to their rank, which did not reduce the opportunities for amorous intrigue, but lent them a piquant touch. Even the modern beholder will smile at these little treasures of illumination, although their literary content may be incomprehensible to him without the text.
Chagall thinks only of the lovers, he makes us forget the more or less daring and exciting circumstances under which they are meeting. From the point of view of the observer the most sacred scenes become trivialities; but Chagall does not observe, he identifies himself with his characters. The piquant ballads become stanzas from the Song of Songs. In his pictures, too, we find realistic secondary figures, but they are merely the earthly counterparts of the lofty events. The lovers sail along, beings from an archaic relief, closely resembling the figures that appear in our dreams and memories. And just as the spaces and inhabitants of our dreams are devoid of any colour to which we can give a name, so Chagall's visions exist in a chromatic scale of black, grey and opalescent white. Yet the spectator imagines he can see in them more midnight blue, starry gold, moonlight-flooded green and shimmering flesh tints than in the gold-framed figures and vistas of the medieval peep-show pictures that glitter with all the colours of the palette.

The Harmonious Synthesis

The directness and freshness that found expression in the Indian-ink drawings are also manifest in the gouaches of this period and in a few oil paintings that resemble gouaches in character. The colours often take the form of patches laid in with great sureness of touch, which mingle so naturally with the graphic components linking or overlaying them that we are struck equally by the plastic effect they produce and by the constructive intelligence to which they bear witness. Often, too, the colours flow into one another and give rise to shapes of atmospheric delicacy.

Chagall has now developed the ability to endow his pictures with a quality so vivid that it impresses itself upon all our senses. There is a gouache showing a blue vessel, in which the shore, the boat with a bridal couple aboard, and a half nude in the foreground, grow so effortlessly and organically in space, the paint is so alive, that they give the beholder the sensation of looking at a dream. The figure of Christ appears again, first in *The Yellow Christ in the Moonlight* (1950) and then in *Christ on the Bridge* (1952).

In the former painting the figure of Christ looking down with raised arms upon a mother and child has more the appearance of bestowing a blessing than of being crucified. The paths of circular and spiral pigment in the background, whose lower offshoots enclose the outlines of the mother and child as well as of the sun, enhance the impression of an embrace, of consolation, lending the picture – even in its abstract plastic values – a physiognomy that is full of ardour and devotion. In these works the power of the pictorial media to express an emotional content through their abstract qualities seems to have reached its ultimate culmination. The pigments grow as naturally in the forms as the juices in the cells of the fruit pulp or the colours in the fabric of a butterfly's wing.

On the occasion of an exhibition of Chagall's latest gouaches at the Galerie Maeght in Paris, a critic wrote:

'...In the pictures painted in exile, in America, I admired the grandeur and abundance of inspiration; but occasionally the ambitiousness of their aims caused a certain strain and awkwardness to appear in their execution; some fundamental harmony seemed to me to be disturbed or at least threatened; in exchanging the felt slippers for the seven league boots our Ariel appeared to have lost the secret of his dance. But no! As soon as we looked at the gouaches we saw that Ariel had not been buried beneath the beard of the prophet or the swarms of the Apocalypse: his whole fantastic skill was there, more alive and sure than ever before – the dance and the song, the thousand and one nights and the thousand and one days. To put it quite plainly: before these new flowers of his art I had to call back to mind the pictures of the visionary, especially those which had deceived me; I had to ask myself whether the effort they showed had been in vain, whether the painter would not one day unite the various phases of his development, all the hours of his life, all the forms of his art and his song, in a harmonious synthesis. I knew that he himself dreamed of this and translated these dreams into poignant drafts. Today I have seen the pictures... Happy painter who in his third youth finds his highest, most perfect and most lasting expression...'

The endeavour to dematerialize paint, to render the surface of the picture precious and significant solely by means of paint – so that the fingers are tempted to touch and feel it, as though this physical contact could place an added enchantment on the senses – may have led Chagall to employ another material which, in its own substance, contains the promise of transformation and relevation. The new technique was painting on clay, which only attains to its poetic existence in the refining heat of the kiln.

'The Echo of an Art at once Close and Remote'

Provence boasts of a ceramic tradition going back to classical antiquity; the neighbouring townlet of Vallauris, made famous by Picasso, lives by its pottery industry. In Vence, too, there are pottery workshops. The vases and jugs that stand in front of the potters' shops, and the painted bowls and plates hanging on the walls, are as much part of the town as its fountains, citadel walls, Roman inscriptions and the scent of its perfume and nougat factories.
One can see the potters busy in their workshops from the street; many a stroller wanders into Serge Ramel's Poterie du Peyra, for the joy of stepping out of the busy, sun-flooded streets into the cellar-like shady room and watching the master moulding cool, damp clay with skilful hands on his potter's wheel.
When Chagall walks into the centre of Vence from his studio, he has to pass at least one of these workshops on his short journey. Knowing how deeply he, whom the world calls a dreamer, is concerned with everything visible, we can imagine how moved he must have been by the example of these craftsmen and the beauty of their handiwork.
Nothing happens without preparation in a world in which things are in a perpetual state of flux and every event is a link in a chain of evolution. Chagall turned to ceramics at a moment when his pictures, especially his gouaches, were developing colours and shapes that resembled those of subtle ceramic painting. If Chagall's early pictures were a testimony to his quest for metaphor in subject and form, the later ones bear witness to the fact that his urge to create metaphors is increasingly concentrated on the expressive potentialities of colour.
When he painted on clay something happened that Chagall may always have wished: the pigments no longer looked as though they had been put on, but as though they had grown organically into the background material, as though they had become one with it. Before his own experiments the painter became the astonished spectator of a process in which the elements of fire and earth were active participants.
In Chagall's ceramics we can distinguish between paintings on round or oval plates and bowls; on vases; on tiles, either singly or fitted together to form larger pictorial surfaces; and ceramic sculptures, which again are developed out of jugs and bowls.

Many of the symbols painted on the clay – the animals' heads, the sun, the moon, the profiles of lovers – seem to have been sketched in with a brush stroke. But the linear quality of these brush drawings is altogether different from the stereotyped patterns of mass-produced pottery. Here, too, Chagall seeks to compel the drawn or painted image, the moulded clay and the glaze into a plastic unity, to create with every piece a unique work of art.
Over and above the simpler linear constructions – which became *peinture* in the course of the ceramic process – Chagall also strove after a more comprehensive form of expression in paint. He may have had before his eyes a kind of ceramic painting capable of vying in plastic richness and sensuous power with his pictures. In fact he succeeded in this medium in transmuting his forms and colours into 'singing matter'. The master potter Serge Ramel, who assisted him in many of his experiments, can testify to the self-willed obstinacy with which Chagall struggled to realize his ideas – often in the teeth of taboos hallowed by tradition. Here again the audacious artist triumphed over the expert who kept to the customary principles of the craft.

The 'subjects' of these ceramic constructions and pictures – like those of Chagall's other works – are not susceptible of literary interpretation. These works draw their power and magic from the unexpected conjunctions of abstract metaphors in colour, from the resuscitation of the accustomed images and their metamorphosis into new formal and spatial relationships. Thrilling configurations penetrate a black that is as transluscent as quartz, a yellow ochre that gleams like amber, a white and a pink that glisten like the interior of a shell. Pigment rubbed on as a dust dissolves in a haze, dots and streaks foam into veils, clouds and undersea shadows, blossom into submarine flora or constellations of dream stars. Faces, bodies, limbs, arms and hands, eyes and lips, emerge from dark and light veinings and reliefs. We understand their language, their joys and sorrows, their songs and predictions, before consciousness has grasped the connexion and meaning of their forms.
The figures and symbols in Picasso's ceramic paintings live with a life that presses outwards from within; they attack the spectator with the lucidity of their appearance that is in a state of constant metamorphosis, with their myriad masks and faces. But they remain attached to their material by an almost imperceptible membrane. They tolerate no aperture, no wound, through which the breath of loving proximity can breathe, the blood of common suffering flow. They take man by his organs of perception and reflection, but leave his heart unmoved. Chagall's images, on the other hand, soar in a world full of mysteries and marvels. They entice the beholder into the world of their agonies and blisses and take possession of him in the whole of his being.

It was only a step from this painted pottery to the ceramic sculptures that developed out of vases and bowls, in which the vessel and the symbols it bears are no longer a background with superimposed forms, but a single sculptural unity. This is manifest in certain vase forms in which the shapes of a cock and a female nude that grow out of the vase are fused into a single mythological being. The spout of the jug and the beak of the cock are one and the same, the vessel's handle is simultaneously the curve of the cock's wing and the bent arm of a woman. On the glazed surface of the sculpture we find motifs such as Chagall once painted on the arms and faces of his actors. Do these works satisfy all the plastic canons of sculpture? Or are they figures taken from the world of pictures that carry the atmosphere of their origin about them like an aureole?
'These few pieces', wrote Chagall, 'these few experiments in pottery are as it were a foretaste, in a sense the outcome of my life in the South, where the importance of this ancient craft can be so clearly felt. Even the earth on which I walk is luminous. It looks at me tenderly, as though it wished to call me. I wanted to handle this earth as the old craftsmen did. I wanted to get away from fortuitous decoration, and remaining within the bounds of ceramics, to breathe into it the echo of an art that is at once close and remote, I had the sudden feeling that this bright earth was calling awake the deaf earth of my far-off hometown.
'But the earth, like the craft itself, does not yield up its secrets so easily. Sometimes the fire releases my "children of sorrow" from the kiln approvingly, but at other times they come out in grotesque and ridiculous shapes. The ancient elements remind me only too well that my means are modest.'

From 1951 on, in addition to his ceramic work, Chagall carved in stone, creating monuments in relief and three-dimensional statues. His materials were marble and light-coloured Rhône stone. We have already spoken of the relief-like structure of the painting in his pen and ink work, which was particularly evident in his illustrations to Boccaccio, in those figures that often look as though carved in stone and whose apparently weather-worn surfaces tempt the spectator to touch them. It would be foolish to deduce from this example a line of succession, as though the one had determined the other. Before many of Chagall's pictures the idea that their creator was experimenting with sculpture would never enter our heads. Faced with these pen and wash drawings we have to correct our preconceived ideas; looking at them we begin to understand why Chagall, in search of ever increasing resistance on the part of his media – even in the manual sphere – should have turned to the most refractory material of all – stone. Did he not see every day from his property at Vence the silent, rugged limestone cliffs of the Baous plateau towering above the vineyards and olive

groves that bordered his park? Were they not bound to inspire him like the greenery in his garden, and the glowing colours of the flowers?
As in the pictures so in the sculptures, one theme seems to take precedence: two figures, often no more than faces, bend towards one another – a man and a woman, a youth and a girl. Sometimes the heads are transmuted into physiognomies full of resignation and painful knowledge, into a silent last meeting between Christ and Mary, or the crowned head of David sinking down over his lyre.
What seemed in the paintings a stony structure engraved with runes, has now become actual stone, and the shapes and figures carved from the stone possess all the qualities we associate with this material – silence, immovability, the mystery that has permeated its substance through the aeons of its growth. The limbs and bodies rarely show an urge to passionate movement, the forms seldom stand forth wilfully from the block, for the most part they are motionless, enclosed volume, their expression is restrained, the surge of movement held in check.

These sculptures of Chagall's resemble early Attic stelae. Only the smile on their faces is not one of astonished wonderment at the glory of a pristine world; it is rather a smile of innocence, wisdom and hints of knowledge drawn from much suffering. Did not the critic Efross, at a time when Chagall was still young in years, say that he was two thousand years old? 'I feel more and more how right Efross was', said Chagall once, as we stood before these sculptures. 'I have never been young in the real sense of the word...'
These figures, which have lost none of their softness and soaring quality through the hardness and heaviness of the stone into which they have been magically transformed, have now become 'plastic' matter in a double sense. They seem to have been taken out of the shell of the pictorial world and set down in the cavern of our real world, where we become their meditative partners. We feel our existence to be something fluid, something striving from an uncertain beginning towards a still uncertain end, which at this instant represents no more than a span of transition between past and future, whose limits grow more fugitive the moment we attempt to establish them more securely. Face to face with these sculptures we take part in a piece of creation; as we look at them and identify ourselves with them we achieve the tranquillity of the forms and beings that slumber in the stone.
Looking at sculptures we are moved by many emotions, the meaning of our origin and destiny is brought to consciousness in a variety of ways: they make us strong and confident, but they can also instil fear and terror by showing us that we are no more than prisoners under the spell of powers beyond the capacity of our understanding and sensibility to apprehend.

In Chagall's sculptures we find a confirmation of something we have believed in at moments of quiet happiness and childlike piety: the miracle of our soul, as it is revealed to us in the grace of loving and being loved.

Visions of a Truer and More Beautiful World

Any collection of comments on the work of a living painter will endeavour to include a reference to his latest productions, in response to the demand to be up-to-date, a stimulus no one can escape. Moreover, every additional work enlarges the total body of material. It is always tempting to conclude a series of biographical notes with the description of a work into which all the currents of the artist's past activity seem naturally to issue.

In fact during the years 1955/56 Chagall produced pictures, including the illustrations to Daphnis and Chloe, in which the painter, then almost seventy, gaily and triumphantly gathered together the modulations, tones and rhythms of his colourful universe, to the discovery and invention of which he had devoted a lifetime of effort. I came upon these paintings in the Galerie Maeght, Paris: delicate and yet powerful works in which colour and form had attained the highest possible degree of animation.

One of these pictures bears the title *The Almond Blossoms*. In front of a hilly landscape crowned by the towers and battlements of medieval Vence, we see in the foreground a still life with a floating, reclining couple, a vase from which grows a tall branch covered with blossoms, and an animal's head emerging from leaves and flowers. The woman's body has become a piece of hillside; it seems solid and yet incorporeal – like the flowers, the fruits and the earth of this landscape when they are touched by the light of the setting sun. The head of the female figure rests in the crook of her arm, her hair turns into a bridal veil. The naked youth beside her has raised his torso and tilted back his head in the act of listening; his hands are stretched out across the body of his beloved towards a book.

This couple in the web of the almond blossoms, which envelops the lemon-yellow crescent of the moon, is more than a central pictorial theme; they symbolize the mystery, the beauty, the hopes and the melancholy of a life-process, of that unending river into which all other streams, brooks and springs are absorbed. The mystery that transforms these two is the mystery of all metamorphosis. Above the couple and the silhouette of the town hover a bird-animal and a garland of leaves, in the oval of which there crouches a flute-playing shepherd.

אשר
שמנה לחמו

This is the landscape of Daphnis and Chloe, the vision of Greece as it appears to the eyes of Chagall. 'The roots of my first home come into contact with the roots of my second home, which helps me to breathe with a smile', said Chagall of the work he produced at Vence.

This picture may outshine in poetic beauty many of those he painted earlier; and yet a certain hesitation restrains our desire to see this particular work, the last of a series, in a special light. Who can say that tomorrow Chagall will not paint a picture that surpasses this 'last' work in artistic and moral radiance?

We have seen how many different layers there are to Chagall's creative effort, and have observed that this painter's evolution does not exhibit any gradual development from tentative first steps to ever-increasing maturity. Chagall's pictures – like the phenomena of nature with their continual alternation of growth and decay – are complete and valid in all their stages and aspects. In exhibitions of his work, such as have recently been held at Hanover and Basle, every room compels the visitor to linger. He feels no urge to hurry through the rooms containing the early works in order to get to the one with the most recent. The early works arouse his amazement just as much as the later. An early work gains by comparison with a later one and the style and character of the later paintings receive an endorsement from their proximity to the earlier.

There are those who assert that Chagall has really painted only one subject in innumerable guises. And yet his *œuvre* astonishes us precisely by its wealth of painterly ideas, by the breadth of its poetic space. It has the power to draw an echo from the most widely disparate zones of our consciousness. The greater variety of subject matter in the pictures of other painters often cramps our consciousness and leaves the organs of the unconscious unsatisfied. Chagall's subject matter, on the other hand, opens and expands our souls and senses. To Chagall the lovers, flowers and animals are not just part of the world, they are the world itself, which achieves ever more intimate expression with every declaration of love and its artistic transfiguration.

Certainly, there is an element of manic possession in the way the painter extorts new forms and facets from his general theme. But his symbols never degenerate into soulless and bloodless hieroglyphs; the daemonism that finds expression in his work does not point away from the plethora of the world into the factitious vistas of the spectre-haunted void. Chagall knows nothing of the dialectical tension between will and impulse that gives a tragic aspect to so much late European art. His work is free from that exacerbated sensibility, that wounded will, whose groans may be heard in many works of the most recent of the moderns. Chagall's fashioning hand and planning mind were guided by love and kindness, and so his work sheds light on the abundance of reality, which embraces more than mere visible appearances. In Chagall, every act of creation discloses a piece of the radiance that shone out of the eyes of God when he created the world in which we live. The worlds of Chagall's imagery are no lost paradises: they find their justification in every loving impulse which men experience in faith and humility. Because the world did not always understand this, it labelled Chagall a dreamer, a teller of fairy tales, a mystic. Chagall has protested against this and declared that he is concerned only with the problems of painting and picture-construction. Nevertheless, he is more than just a picture-maker: the impulse that drove him to record his visions in area, colour and form was set in motion by an inner purpose. His aim was to seek something that had been lost, to depict it and to enable people to believe in it. His paintings are symbols of certainties more profound than themselves.

The question whether Chagall's paintings can make themselves felt in a time when all deceptive glitter and all romantic hopes have been stripped away by the memory of the blackest horrors in history has already answered itself. When we came to his pictures with our cares and worries we discovered that in them he had suffered our sorrows before us. May it not be that in his new paintings – once more a long way ahead of us – he has recorded a world, a time, a life in which we no longer believe, translating it into the allegorical guise of poetry, which, while it is derived from life, is more durable, more pregnant, more potent than life? Chagall's pictures grip us for the simple reason that they prove there are still people capable of rousing visions of a truer, more beautiful world.

When I came to Vence for the second time, with my notes on Chagall in my travelling bag, my first visit was once again to the painter. It was a May Sunday, early in the afternoon. The fronds of the tall palms had been frozen in the last hard winter and hung limply like strips of brown bast. The greater expanse of air and the unfiltered light caused the house, which last summer had lain entangled in the greenery of the park, to stand out more detached from its surroundings. The effects of the long journey and uncertainty as to whether the approaching reunion would confirm the happy impression of the first meeting aroused in me a disquiet as to whose cause I was at the time uncertain.

For many years the memory of his pictures had been to me like entirely personal recollections; I had never missed an opportunity of tracking down an unknown painting by his hand. The phenomenon Chagall had taken possession of me, I saw the works of the other great moderns only in relation to his. But did this entitle me to expect a special human response from the painter? Even the unaccustomed sun, the extravagant blossoms around me and the scent of the nearby rose garden could not set me free from my qualms.

At this moment Chagall came down the steps from his studio. He was in a cheerful mood and stretched out his hand to me in greeting. The kindliness that radiated from his face and movements immediately banished my fears.

'I'm still the same Chagall', he cried. 'There's nothing new, nothing remarkable about me!' He waved me into the house. An instant later we were sitting by the fireplace at the open window. This time the picture of the lovers round the Eiffel Tower was hanging in full light, undimmed by any sunblind, curtain, or awning of foliage.

Chagall was wearing a thin purple corduroy jacket and a corn-yellow shirt. His face seemed to me softer, more mobile than at our first meetings; at moments the gestures of his hands and the play of his facial expression had the charm of a woman's. He filled two glasses with red wine and raised his to me. 'I'm glad to see you again!' Then, as he put down the glass again: 'C'est bon, le doux vin de France!'

During my journey to Vence and the short break in Paris I had been surrounded by nothing but unrest and vibrant life; in Chagall's presence the music of the world was tuned to a softer, more allusive note that made even the familiar and apparently insignificant important.

I told him what pleasure I had derived from my preoccupation with his work, and that I was sorry the undertaking was nearing its end, in so far as it could

ever be at an end; for the more intensely I had pursued them, the more questionable my efforts had appeared to me. I felt like starting all over again on the basis of the insights I had now acquired.
'Vous êtes trop gentil', replied Chagall. 'I don't know what I have done to deserve your interest at all. I can well understand what you say about your work; every picture confronts me with new problems and demands greater efforts from me. I don't know what is to come, either in my own work or in painting as a whole. I feel I am at the beginning every time I stand in front of a white canvas. And then colour! A lifetime is not long enough to realize its potentialities. It's impossible to put my aims into words. If I try to do so nevertheless, the truth of what I say is only a *vérité émotionelle*, as Lionello Venturi once phrased it who had also come to question me. So my words are only to be understood in the context in which they are uttered; it is a mistake to take a painter's remarks literally.'
I protested that a word may often substantiate the concord that exists between an artist's work and his life as a man. I told him how, while I was in Paris, I had visited his old studio in *La Ruche*, in the Rue Dantzig. In the room he had once occupied there now lived a young painter from Perpignan and his even younger, slim and pretty wife. They had to pay 10,000 francs a month for the studio – a price whose value was ten times as high as the rent he had paid before the First World War. They got along as best they could. They certainly did not worship the spirits of those who had occupied these rooms before them, and yet the name Chagall and those of his former studio neighbours had become watchwords for them. In the work of this painter there were to be seen once more lovers and animals in a dream landscape, once more a young painter was struggling to realize his pictorial visions, achieve plastic values on a flat surface, and the harmony of form and content.
'Everything may change in our demoralized world', replied Chagall vigorously, 'except the heart, man's love and his striving to know the divine. Painting, like all poetry, has a part in the divine; people feel this today just as much as they used to. What poverty surrounded my youth, what trials my father had with us nine children. And yet he was always full of love and in his way a poet. Through him I first sensed the existence of poetry on this earth. After that I felt it in the nights, when I looked into the dark sky. Then I learnt that there was also another world. This brought tears to my eyes, so deeply did it move me.'

Chagall had made more use of German than at our first meetings. In his mouth the language sounded soft and melodious. For all its liveliness, his facial expression was reserved, as though after every thought he withdrew into that cavern in which he places the figures in his pictures.

'Young people may feel the same thing nowadays and express it in their own way', Chagall said after a while. 'They should only take care not to make of their artistic work a profession based on speculation and calculation. Love, poetry and the divine cannot be cooked up according to a system. Only think of Leonardo's desperate attempts to get to the secret of poetry through scientific experiments. These testimonies in his hand move us as documents of a tragic endeavour; but what count are his few paintings and his drawings, there alone he proves himself a genius. But it is precisely the other thing – speculation and calculation – that has own pupils. That's what the modern world, with its hate and war, lives by. It has gone so far that strategists and the inventors of murderous weapons are called geniuses – what a misunderstanding of the concept genius!

The conversation was interrupted by the appearance of the old housekeeper, who informed us with a gesture that tea was ready in the next room. 'Isn't Madame Chagall joining us?' Chagall enquired. The housekeeper told him that Madame was in the studio. He smiled. 'The moment I leave my studio my wife goes in to tidy up a bit.' We strolled into the next room, chatting as we went, and sat at the laid table. Chagall poured out the tea. He drank from a glass in a chased silver holder, such as the Russians love, I from a nut-brown ceramic bowl. There was sliced sponge cake and very sweet jam. In response to my enquiry Chagall told me about the two trips to Greece he had made while working on the prints for *Daphnis and Chloe*. For a while we both rhapsodized on the beauty of the Aegean islands, of their colours and their light. 'What poetry there is in early Greek sculpture', cried Chagall. 'I don't feel the same about the later work...'

I thought of Chagall's sculptures with the archaic smile they have regained. On a low wall-cupboard behind Chagall's back stood one of his ceramic sculptures, ochre in colour, unglazed and unpainted: a reclining nude terminating in a deep bowl. A touch of Greek light seemed to be reflected in this light-coloured baked clay, these gently moulded forms, the smile on the lips, and the limbs. Poets have sung of the *air grec* that pervades the landscape around Vence.

Chagall must have noticed that my eyes were resting on this sculpture. He got up, moved to one side, and turned it slowly round, as though to show me how every angle revealed new formal relationships, how the limbs and body of the female figure flowed into the concavity of the bowl. Did not early Etruscan statues of women also carry bowls in their hands?

It was fascinating to watch Chagall with his 'children of sorrows', as he had once called his ceramic works. I felt a sudden desire to see him in his studio, and told him so.

'What do you hope to get out of that? It's just a room like any of the others here.' When I repeated my request he led me into the workroom that stood next to the house.

'Voilà! C'est tout!' he said, opening the door. Again he made an apologetic movement with his shoulders. I had seen enough studios to have grown to value their inspiring atmosphere. The studio of the painter, whose task is to transmute earthly matter into poetic substance, will always be plain and utilitarian. As a rule, any aesthetic decoration as an intentional stimulant is liable to reduce his power of artistic transformation. This does not mean that such a studio does not contain some of the same mystery that radiates from its occupant's pictures.

The room before me – small in relation to the size of many of Chagall's paintings – revealed this sobriety, so that I felt no surprise as I entered it. At first I thought that I was looking through a narrow door in the opposite wall into an adjoining room. Only when the bright oblong filled with life did I realize that what I had taken to be an opening was really a tall mirror reaching down to the floor, in which the room and our figures were reflected.
Close to the white-curtained window there extended a large work table; the rest of the room was filled by several small tables and shelves piled with papers, pencils, brushes and tubes. Vases and vessels stood all over the place with more brushes sprouting from them, and in between bottles and tin pots. On the walls hung photographs of pictures, including some of Chagall's own; I noticed a colour reproduction of *The Birthday*, cut out of a copy of *Life* and yellowed by the sunlight. On the shelves lay and stood books, sculptures and ceramics. Powder colours were heaped on tiles placed neatly side by side. I could see no easels; pictures stood in rows, leaning with their faces to the wall. A long canvas was stretched on one wall – a painting in progress, showing a circus scene with a large number of figures, animals, harlequins and acrobats. In front of this picture we stopped.

The background with its rich scale of blues, greys and violets shot through by darker shadows, seemed to be already dry. A galaxy of figures appeared from its depths and wreathed themselves round the principal figures in the foreground. Their colours had been put on to the more delicately painted ground as though with a palette knife, and they now flashed, glowed and flamed like necklaces of rubies, emeralds and pearls. The lozenges of colour on the harlequin's costume seemed to break away from their bearer and lead a life of their own with a new organization and meaning.

Chagall pointed first to one, than to another part of the picture. 'I want to keep the paint as lively as possible, des couleurs fraîches et brutes...' He pointed to the great angel's head floating in the upper right-hand corner, a dominant patch of strong ultramarine glowing with an inner life. Then he indicated other blue shapes to show how they corresponded to one another. The hand ran over the lozenges of paint put on with the palette knife. 'As though phosphorescent...', he remarked. Then the hand divided up the surface into curves, sketched in the triangle formed by the main elements of the composition, and returned to the colours. At one point they glowed as though sprayed on, elsewhere they struck a fuller note. During this 'explanation' I could see that Chagall was thinking only of the construction of the forms, of the musical distribution of the chromatic values. The few words he uttered, and his gestures in front of the picture, were more of a monologue, as though, after his brief absence from the painting, he had to render an account of the progress so far made. Not once did he speak of the subject of the picture, the circus. And yet this painting was especially rich in that lustre which makes the arena occupied by harlequins and clowns appear a symbol of poetry, of the 'other world'.
'What do you think of the picture?' Chagall enquired all of a sudden. Was this question asked out of politeness, or was he really interested in my 'first impression'? After a few moments' thought, I suggested that the painting was an attempt to concentrate still further on the expressive value of colour. That the spectator felt compelled to think in terms of colour sensations. Yet even in this picture colour could not be divorced from form. I pointed to outlines that were welded into the structure, into the interaction of colours, like veins shimmering through skin. I praised the richness of the themes: all the motifs of his earlier creations were there, transformed in a spirit of playfulness, even of virtuosity. I thought of the example of a soloist in a piano concerto who gives his best in free improvization after the cadenza, in which all the themes of the composition have been gathered up.
Chagall listened attentively. 'I'm trying to do something new, but I don't know whether I shall succeed. Simple tasks no longer attract me, fundamentally they never did: Now I can only think of more comprehensive pictorial constructions...'

He stepped back from the picture and turned towards the open window. The sky above the park was a stormy blue-grey, the foliage of the pines and the underbrush velvety black, in between the May green of the new leaves flashed impetuously, every shape looking as though chased in metal.
Chagall's expression had become impersonal; the intensity of his gaze made his face appear tauter and more serious. He seemed to have forgotten my presence.

Had he been aware of it at all? I had tried many ways of coming closer to Chagall's world of images. Until now I had imagined that the surest and most revealing would be through Chagall the man. But at this instant I realized – and this realization was vouchsafed me through the proximity of Chagall the man – that there was only one way, the way contained in the pictures themselves.

Epilogue – ten years later

It is some years since I was last a guest in Chagall's white house in Vence. But the memory is as fresh as though it was yesterday. It is only intense encounters which thus establish themselves in the memory. In the garden Chagall's grandchildren were playing noisily, and the twelve-year-old David, Chagall's son from his second marriage, kicked a football against the whitewashed wall on which the painter had scratched a large animal.

How much Chagall needs his familiar environment on the Côte d'Azur I had been able to observe when I met him in an exclusive Roman hotel on the Via Veneto, where everything angered and irritated him. 'For heaven's sake, let's get back to Vence!' he exclaimed. And yet Chagall loves the Eternal City as few people do. On this visit to Rome he had been particularly interested in the Etruscan Museum in the Villa Giulia. He spoke with enthusiasm of the sculptures and frescoes at Tarquinia, Veii and Cerveteri.

In those days, when Chagall was asked about his plans for the future, he dismissed the question with a weary gesture. 'I work all day long. When I get up I think to myself, what shall I do; when I go to bed in the evening I'm worried that I haven't been able to do more. It's always the same!'

One must call to mind such resigned remarks in order to appreciate fully the uniquely important works that he has produced in the meantime. The wish: 'Je cherche un grand mur!', which he expressed at that time as he walked past the wall in his garden on which he had scratched the *grafitti*, had been fulfilled. In fact we might call the intervening period the 'Decade of the Large Wall', if we include the stained-glass windows: the window for the Unesco Building in New York, the windows for Jerusalem, the painting for the Frankfurt opera-house, and finally the ceiling of the Paris opera-house.

How many isms have been created during these years by solicitous public relations men, only to sink into oblivion, while the works of Chagall, as he proceeds from task to task, bear witness to a refreshed and rejuvenated genius. His works demonstrate the highest artistic maturity, which can never become adacemic or even sterile because in the world of Chagall's pictures childhood, youth and the wisdom of age always enter into a new, fruitful synthesis. Perhaps no one can see what youth and beauty are so clearly as a convalescent, for whom the world is renewed and deepened with every morning, while 'reality' becomes increasingly a metaphor.

Of the plans that preoccupied Chagall during the ensuing years, the first one, which was also the one that it would have been geographically easiest for the painter to carry out, prospered least. Even during my first visit to Vence there was already talk of Chagall decorating a Chapelle du Calvaire situated near Vence on a hill surrounded by greenery and approached by a path lined with small chapels. I still remember a conversation with the mayor of Vence – an Alsatian who, with his white goatee beard, looked like a retired Prussian ship's officer – and the enthusiasm which this sober man displayed when he spoke of the 'chapel on the enchanted hill' which 'my friend Chagall is going to decorate'. Unfortunately all attempts to realize this project, to which Chagall had become so attached, proved vain.

Chagall thought first of decorating the little church with murals, in the manner of the religious cycles painted after 1950. But to accommodate such a series of paintings would have involved rebuilding the church, and this the authorities were not prepared to undertake. A frieze of tapestries was also considered, likewise a series of ceramics. (The cartoon for a tapestry is now in the Stedelijk-Museum in Amsterdam.) The possibility of stained-glass windows was also discussed. Regrettable as it is that the plan, which received support from so many sides, was never executed, the multiplicity of possibilities which the painter had to consider in the course of the years, and which found expression in many sketches and samples, had forced him to go deeper into the problems of glass-painting and the mural. Of the few pictures completed, the first, *The Creation of Man* (118 1/2" × 78 3/4") was exhibited in Paris in 1958.

The composition of the picture is dominated by the colours blue and yellow, the colours of coolness, of beginning. The blue with its churned-up texture symbolizes the power of the primordial waters, its movements the breath of the Creator. The sky is a pure glow of richly modulated golden-yellow. Out of the blue emerges the youthful figure of the angel, carrying still unawakened man into his future destiny. The outlines of the first human couple shimmer into existence – this is the beginning of history. But Adam and Eve are still totally enveloped in a poetic atmosphere: it is the meeting before knowledge.

In the top right-hand quarter of the picture the rotating sun forms a mighty counterpoint, disks of carmine and vermilion tending towards violet. Vast rays vibrate within the colours of the rainbow and perform concentric motions. In this 'other existence' angels and prophets are gathered, King David plucks his harp. The posture of the Saviour on the cross proclaims the future redemption of the world. Behind the merely hinted outline of a temple there glows in unearthly white a more spiritual sun, which conceals the figure of God. Two hands hold aloft the tables of the Law. This cosmogony, in which the Christian is included but does not dominate, has absorbed all myths of the Creation in its radiance. It is Chagall's hymn to the energy of the ever self-renewing life with which, even in this violated world, the believer is filled. With this picture Chagall's art loses its merely aesthetic character, even though there is no area of it that does not satisfy the highest artistic demands.

Collaboration on two new projects was to prove more successful. One was to decorate the church of Notre Dame de Toute Grâce in the mountain spa of Plâteau d'Assy. The art-loving Father Couturier had on previous occasions called in important artists of France — Bonnard, Rouault, Matisse, Braque and Léger. Chagall created for the baptistery of this church two ceramic reliefs and two stained-glass windows with angels. After this he was invited to design two windows for Metz cathedral which were to harmonize in colour and architectonic rhythm with the existing sixteenth-century windows. Chagall drew inspiration for his new stained-glass window designs from a typical 'Chagall motif', a green donkey in a medallion window of the aisle that he had discovered while studying Chartres cathedral. Whereas in the case of Father Couturier's church 'bright' windows were required, in Metz Chagall was able to work with his usual more intense scale of colours, which even in his earlier pictures had already had something of the glow of medieval stained-glass.

While he was working on these windows, of which up to the present only one has been completed, Chagall received a commission to design windows for a new synagogue near Jerusalem. Chagall felt the windows he had designed up to then to be a kind of overture to larger and more comprehensive works. After completing the first window in Metz in June 1959 he remarked: 'That is like an embryo, still entirely undeveloped, but now I can sense possibilities . . . It was the same when I began work on the Bible.'

The initiative in commissioning Chagall to execute twelve stained-glass windows for the synagogue of the Hebrew University Medical Center at Ain-Karem, a few miles west of Jerusalem in the mountains of Judaea, originated from the Hadassah, a women's charitable organization in the United States. They were exhibited at the Museum of Modern Art in New York before being installed in Jerusalem. The Hadassah is concerned with the building of hospitals and universities in the young State of Israel. The synagogue, which stands in the centre of a modern policlinic, is a rectangular building with a tower shaped like a lantern. The twelve windows – twelve is a sacred number to the Jews – form the walls of this tower. Each window is three metres high and two and a half metres wide.

Chagall chose the theme of the twelve tribes of Israel that are extolled by Moses in the verses of Genesis and Deuteronomy. Mosaic law forbids portrayal of the human figure as the image and likeness of God. Therefore Chagall was compelled to employ appropriate symbols for each tribe and the patriarchs representing them: animals, plants and fruits, sacred implements, the symbols for the heavenly bodies, for the tables of the Law and the commandments, for the holy places and temples, and finally the emblems and colours for the elements and areas that house these symbols.

Thus we find in the windows the lion as the heraldic beast of Judah, the ass as the animal of the tribe of Issachar, the golden eagle and the crowned horse as the symbols of the tribe of Gad, the slender hind, emblem of the tribe of Naphtali. We see Noah's dove, the grapes and the olive-tree symbolizing peace, and the viper, symbol of war and conflict. The three- and the seven-branched candlestick, the resounding ram's horn, the breaking wave and the fish – there is not a single object that is not a religious symbol. Shining forth out of the blue sky to crown it all are the eye of God and two hands holding the tables of the Law.

Every window glows in a different colour of the rainbow, each colour corresponding to the character and nature of the particular tribe. Marine blue symbolizes the atmosphere of the Creation which surrounds the emblems of the oldest tribe, that of Reuben; yellow, the symbol of light and spirituality, is ascribed to the intermediary between God and the people, Levi. The dramatic purple reflects the battles in the history of the tribe of Judah, while bright-green is to be seen as the sign of the peace and serenity which – according to the Scriptures – are the lot of the tribe of Issachar.

In his earlier pictures Chagall had already so humanized his bestiary that it was not difficult for him now to let the human shine through the emblems of the sacred. We have only to look at the windows as 'landscapes' or 'still-lifes' in order to realize how the eye which created them is manifested in the forms of the plants and animals, the mountains, clouds and architecture, and with the eye the painter's heart, which is a believing heart. Of the windows in Jerusalem the French critic Jean Leymarie wrote: 'Man is absent from them only in order to be absorbed in the universe.' One might also say that precisely in the truth, goodness and humility that speak from the colours and forms – expressive qualities that continue into the individual line, into the detail of the lively areas of colour – human participation is doubly manifest.

Thus the richness of the windows unfolds itself to the spectator directly; there is no need for the detour via theological speculation. Even if the aesthetic sensation leads the spectator on to read and meditate on the passages in the Bible and the religious truths that they proclaim, the knowledge derived from pure contemplation nevertheless remains primary, a knowledge which, as in Chagall's pictures, raises the profane and the sacred onto a higher plane where they become fused.

Unlike the stained-glass windows created by Léger and Matisse, whose effect springs solely from the contrast between pure tones, Chagall has sought to use stained glass in a more traditional manner which, however, thanks to his poetic conception of expressive colour and form, he has set free from its centuries-old stagnation. He has made a careful study of the old stained-glass windows at Chartres and knows how brittle glass can be compelled to take on the brilliance of nobler and more precious materials. Thus the windows of the synagogue flash as though inlaid with diamonds, rubies and emeralds. This brings them close to the medieval vision of a celestial Jerusalem, which the mystics saw as standing on a foundation of precious stones. And did not Jehovah, as he handed over the tables of the Law, command Moses to make a 'breastplate of judgment', that is to say a work of art? 'And thou shalt make the breastplate of judgment with cunning work; after the work of the ephod thou shalt make it; of gold, of blue and of purple, and of scarlet, and of fine twined linen, shalt thou make it. Foursquare it shall be . . . And thou shalt set in it settings of stones, even four rows of stones: the first row shall be a sardius, a topaz, and a carbuncle. And the second row shall be an emerald, a sapphire, and a diamond. And the third row a ligure, an agate, and an amethyst. And the fourth row a beryl, and an onyx, and a jasper . . . And the stones shall be with the names of the children of Israel, twelve, according to their names, like the engravings of a signet; every one with his name shall they be according to the twelve tribes.'

Chagall worked on the windows for more than two years. On the occasion of the consecration of the synagogue in February 1962 he said: 'I have given concrete expression to that which people nowadays call religious, by bearing in mind the great ancient creations of the Semitic peoples. And I hope that in so doing I have stretched out my hand to the friends of culture, the poets and the artists of the neighbouring peoples.'

Chagall's next work was a window for the United Nations Building in New York, dedicated to the memory of the Secretary of UNO, Dag Hammarskjöld, who died in an aeroplane crash in 1961 after dedicating his life and labours to the maintenance of peace in the world. The theme of peace also finds expression in the window. The dominant colour is blue, symbolizing life and peace. Peace is also embodied by the angel soaring out of a bunch of flowers in the centre of the picture and bending down towards a child. On the right-hand side there appear the prophets and martyrs who gave their lives for peace. The left-hand side is filled with figures engaged in the fight for peace, and below them a mother puts her arms protectively round her child. As in the case of the later work, the ceiling of the Paris Opéra, Chagall refused any fee for this large window.

Before turning to the Opéra ceiling, we must consider another work that forms a transition. This is the mural, *Commedia dell'Arte,* in the foyer of the new Frankfurt theatre, the scale of which (99¼" × 151½") exceeds that of any other picture from preceding decades. When the theatre committee were considering which painters and sculptors they might call upon for the decoration of the theatre, they had the courage to go straight to two artists of international renown: Henry Moore and Chagall. To begin with, the committee considered purchasing Chagall's picture *The Big Circus* of 1956. When this proved impossible, they succeeded in persuading the artist to paint a variation on this theme. The *Commedia dell'Arte* was completed in 1959. Up to the ceremonial opening of the theatre, the work was housed in the Städelsche Kunstinstitut. Now it delights the guests strolling about the foyer during the interval, who are treated also to a sculpture by Moore and the *Suns* on the ceilings of the long corridors, a continuous frieze of brass drums by Zoltan Kemeny.

'The benevolent and the critical, the enthusiastic, the disappointed and the indignant spectator – they can all seek their likeness as in a mirror. They will find it,' said the artist in his address of greeting. 'The figures of the Italian *commedia dell'arte* are present today in every theatre: Pantalone and Pulcinella, Arlecchino and Colombina . . . Nowadays, of course, Colombina, the delicate little dove, has a fixed contract, and Arlecchino is entitled to a pension. Pegasus disguised as a unicorn still flies with butterfly wings over the heads of the audience. Bellerophon has become a stage-manager. He has survived the fall from Olympus. The *commedia dell'arte*, which means the world, fills the horizon; the dense wind of dreams blows gently and a thousand years are like a sleep. All the happiness that lies in colours is spread out here; not only Pegasus, the whole picture has wings on which it flies with us into the kingdom of fairy tales, where everything is easy, relaxed and self-evident. Balls and people soar through the air, the law of gravity has been abrogated. In very truth a divine comedy!'

Forty years earlier, Chagall had painted his first picture of acrobats. A very realistic impression, in the manner of the Fauves, without any symbolic associations. The theme of the circus, of acrobats and women bare-back riders, reappears in his *oeuvre* every decade. We recall Chagall's stage décor and mural paintings for the Yiddish Theatre in Moscow of 1921. Did not the physicist Einstein enunciate at the beginning of the twenties the almost Chagallian proposition that when one performs an experiment intended to demonstrate the earth's gravity, one never knows whether the experimental object is attracted by the earth or whether the space surrounding this object does not make a movement upwards, which, from the point of view of physics, amounts to the same thing?

Chagall is not an intellectual painter; equally he cannot be called naive either as a man or a painter. Rather one can speak in his case of an extremely subtle creative intelligence which seeks to combine unheard-of coloristic refinement with the audacity of new compositional constellations. Every artist strives to be 'original' in the double sense of inventing and of going back to the origin of things. He feels compelled to seek along the path of the multi-layered, ramified and complex to gain a grasp of the simple. He can do this, however, only if he has the courage to break away from the familiar; he must first create for himself the basis from which to launch his assault on the new and then, after completing the work, abandon it again. This distinguishes him from the intellectual, whose dialectical endeavours operate exclusively with the existent, who seeks to pervert the simple and to replace the truly original by false 'originality'.

Rather, Chagall is a man of knowledge; he knows a great deal, he keeps himself informed about everything that shows any connexion with the work on which he is at any given moment engaged. He reads a great deal; he has things read to him or translated for him. But when he stands in front of the empty canvas, he forgets everything he has heard or read – which does not rule out the possibility that while he is painting it may unexpectedly reappear in an altered form. Thus we are entitled to regard the *Commedia dell'Arte* as a polyphonous, complex organism in which, as in an 'Art of the Fugue', there are canons, reversals and reflections.

In composition the mural constitutes a triptych. In classical antiquity the stage was a triptych, so were many medieval altar-pieces. The conductor in the centre of the upper edge of the picture occupies exactly the place in which the Supreme Judge appears. The circus arena as part of a circle is a symbol of the earth and the universe, the balls take up the circular form, the ladder represents the connexion between the two worlds. If we turn the picture round, the earth becomes the sky, the air water, from which the outlines of Vitebsk shimmer out as though in a dream. We can read in Bachofen that in antiquity circus games were always credited with a sacred significance. There was no acrobatic exercise, no gymnastic appliance, no dance figure that did not have a religious or mythological meaning. 'The link between circus games and water emerges everywhere', writes Bachofen; elsewhere the investigator of matriarchal cultures quotes a statement by Cassiodorus: 'The effect of circus games lies in the fact that they equate the customs of the people with those of the birds.'

There is nothing to prevent us from interpreting the signs on Chagall's picture as 'archetypal symbols'. The past is simultaneously the present; the moon-sickle a symbol of becoming and passing away; we find the ass's head as a symbol of tellurian potency among the Hebrews, the Egyptians, the Greeks and the Romans. The cock – by contrast with the passive feminine primordial basis of being – is the incarnation of the non-material, spiritual and aggressive, the destructive. The sacred cow, winged Pegasus and circus animal are transformed into one single beast; the acrobats take the place of angels. The acrobat with the outstretched arms is at the same time Christ, the harlequin is both the Fool and Adam, Eve is also Mary, the book in her hands the symbol of poetry.

If we were to ask Chagall whether he had consciously chosen one of these possible affinities, he would smile an ingenuously knowing smile and say: Perhaps, or perhaps not! The substance of poetry cannot be broken down into its component parts like a chemical solution. The boundaries remain fluid, there are many different strata. What remains is the astonished silence!

The ceiling of the Paris Opéra must be regarded as the consummation of Chagall's efforts to achieve a great representational mural. This vast dome of the Palais Garnier, divided from the outset into twelve segments and framed by richly gilded stucco, had depended up to the present upon its sole decoration, the enormous chandelier. The wall-paintings by Jules-Eugène Lenepveu with their pallid grey nudes and mythological emblems representing the 'hours and the muses of day and night' were so submerged in the dusty décor of the theatre, that no visitor can have taken the trouble to give them a glance. And yet the architect Garnier, whose genius is today becoming recognized once more, dreamt of a ceiling 'enlivened with patches of colour'. The initiative in realizing the architect's wish more than half a century after his death originally came from André Malraux, the new Minister of Culture in the de Gaulle era.

After he had finished work on the stained-glass windows in Jerusalem, Chagall was asked to design the stage sets for a ballet performance of Ravel's *Daphnis and Chloe.* Both 'the General' and his 'Minister of State for Cultural Affairs' – Malraux's official title – were present at the gala performance. During the interval of this performance it occurred to Malraux that the painter of these magical settings would also be capable of giving the interior of the opera-house a new face. When this wish was conveyed to Chagall, he at first hesitated before the monumental task – after all, it involved painting two hundred square metres of ceiling. Finally the painter, then 77 years old, agreed.

Chagall's iconography has always borne witness to a fruitful synthesis between tradition and forward-looking poetic *élan.* He must have been the only painter of the 'Ecole de Paris' who would have dared to evolve a pictorial vision of 'gay irony and more profound significance', which at the same time willingly subordinates itself to the pompous architecture dating from the time of Napoleon III.

Since Lenepveu's ceiling-painting was to be left intact, it had been agreed that the twelve segments of the new dome should be made of plastic and fitted, when ready, ten centimetres beneath the old painting. Chagall decided to take as subjects for the twelve fields famous ballets and operas proclaiming the Song of Songs of love. The choice of colours was determined in each case by the poetic atmosphere of the music.

In Chagall's painting, the colours have always stood for particular spiritual and sensual values. Blue symbolized peace and hope, green love, red and yellow mystic ecstasy and elegiac rapture, while white represented the purity of bridal innocence. Thus Mozart's angel soars out of the blue background of the ceiling, protecting the world of the *Magic Flute*. Blue too are the outlines and cupolas of the city of Moscow that surround the figures from Mussorgsky's *Boris Godunov*. A multi-layered green forms the background to Wagner's *Tristan and Isolde* and Berlioz's *Romeo and Juliet*. Stravinsky's *Firebird* blazes out in red and yellow, so do Ravel's *Daphnis and Chloe*, Tchaikovsky's *Swan Lake* and the background figures in Adam's *Giselle*. The outlines of Debussy's *Pélleas and Mélisande* stand out like jewels from a refulgent white.

Between the tutelary spirits, muses, angels and lovers, the half-human half-animal beings and the bunches of flowers, appear the architectural monuments of Paris: the Eiffel Tower, the Opéra, the Arc de Triomphe. The domed churches might also be those of Vitebsk. Thus the Russian and the French worlds are combined in this poetic cosmos. The painting is the gift of Chagall, the Frenchman by choice, to his new homeland.

Out of a hundred designs Chagall had chosen those which came closest to his conception of music. The first sketches consisted of coloured scraps of paper stuck to cardboard. In the next sketches the patches are dabbed-in with pastels and the outlines of the figures and symbols emerge from them. In conversations with friends the painter expressed his idea of the meaning of his 'domes'. As in his earlier pictures, here too he has tried to give his colours the organic quality of a bunch of flowers. A dome is a curve without beginning and without end. A bunch of flowers is a kind of dome in which every flower has its particular colour and radiance. Finally everything grows together into an organic *ensemble* of fragrance, beauty and expression. The eternal themes of the music are contained within the colours of the bouquet. 'I like my painting to remain free from excessive rhetoric' is a remark which Chagall made while working on the ceiling-painting. And he always had flowers standing near him while painting.

To begin with, the workshops of the Gobelins factory in Paris were placed at Chagall's disposal. When these proved to be too small, he continued his work in an airship hangar built by Eiffel. The huge segments were transported to the Opéra by lorry. The ceremonial opening of the redecorated opera-house took place on 23 September 1964. Ravel's *Daphnis and Chloe* was presented on the stage. The power of poetry enabled the mystical Hasidic world of Chagall to be combined in the most fruitful manner with the lucid Mediterranean world of Ravel.

In the foreword to the two de luxe volumes devoted to Chagall's lithographs, the printer Fernand Mourlot gives an account of how Chagall feels himself to be a craftsman as soon as he sets foot in the dusty printing workshop in the 13th Arrondissement. But it also describes how he is continually filled with creative unrest. If he has to wait for the lithographic ink to dry on a stone before the trial pull can be made, he immediately embarks upon a new work in order to try out other possibilities. Similarly, while he was working on the murals and the stained-glass windows, he produced a series of oil paintings, gouaches and lithographs. We may mention the oil painting *The Lovers* (1963) and the gouache *Circus* (1964).

The old subjects merely form the scaffolding for possible experiments with new colours and compositions. With these 'variations' Chagall takes up formal problems such as arise in contemporary 'abstract' painting. In these 'pictures of light and joy', as Julien Cain has called them, the painter's wish 'to create sublime forms and permeate them with subtle refinement' is never wholly assuaged. In the last resort, he wishes his pictures to be judged in terms of the 'alchemy of colour' and does not want to be stereotyped as a 'Jewish painter of fairy-tale worlds'.

How great is his contribution to the modern print may be seen by his latest series of lithographs, particularly the sequence *Daphnis and Chloe* (1962). Here interpretation of the figurative element is unnecessary; the content has become all colour, all poetry, and each print reveals its own special melodic system and atmosphere. Thus Chagall changes from day to day. He lives not only in the ever-changing world, he also lives in the world of art, of old and of so-called new art. It would certainly not be fruitful to try to trace 'influences' in his latest works. This will be the task of future seminars on art history; Chagall does not think much of them. A well-known English newspaper criticized the author of this book for not having made sufficient effort to track down possible 'models' that might have influenced Chagall while he was working on his last lithographs – the part played by Odilon Redon's pictures, for example. When I asked Chagall about such possible models, he looked at my daughter and said: 'What rubbish! When you begot this charming child were you thinking about Odilon Redon?' He smiled his almost shamefaced harlequin's smile, and all questions as to 'whence?' and 'whither?' lost their tormenting acuteness before the power of suggestion exercised by this vital moment in the garden of his property in Vence.

List of Plates

COLOUR PLATES

I The Sabbath, 1909. Oil, $35\frac{3}{8}$" × $31\frac{3}{8}$". Wallraf-Richartz-Museum (Haubrich Collection), Cologne.

II Me and My Village, 1911. Oil, $75\frac{5}{8}$" × $59\frac{5}{8}$". Museum of Modern Art (Mrs. Simon Guggenheim Fund), New York. (Courtesy of Joh. Enschedé en Zonen, Haarlem, Netherland)

III Rabbi, 1912. Oil, 52" × $36\frac{5}{8}$". Private Collection, Krefeld.

IV Gate to the Cemetery, 1917. Oil, $34\frac{1}{4}$" × 27". Coll. Mme. Ida Meyer-Chagall, Berne.

V The Girl Acrobat, 1930. Oil, $20\frac{1}{2}$" × $25\frac{5}{8}$". Musée National d'Art Moderne, Paris.

VI The Bride and Groom of the Eiffel Tower, 1938–39. Oil, $58\frac{1}{4}$" × $57\frac{1}{8}$". Pierre Matisse Gallery, New York.

VII King David, 1950–51. Oil, $76\frac{3}{8}$" × $51\frac{1}{8}$". Owned by the Artist.

VIII The Falling Angel, 1923–33–47. Oil, $58\frac{1}{4}$" × $65\frac{3}{8}$". Kunstmuseum, Basle.

IX The Sleigh, 1943. Gouache, $20\frac{1}{8}$" × $29\frac{1}{8}$". Coll. Mme Ida Meyer-Chagall, Berne.

X The Banks of the Seine, 1953. Oil, $31\frac{1}{8}$" × $26\frac{3}{4}$". Private Collection, Paris.

XI Red Nude, 1954–55. Oil, $39\frac{3}{8}$" × $28\frac{3}{4}$". Collection M. Rosensaft, Montreux.

XII The Tribe of Asher, 1961. Window for the synagogue of the Hebrew University Medical Center near Jerusalem, 133" × $98\frac{3}{4}$".

BLACK AND WHITE PLATES

1 Family, 1908. Oil, $21\frac{1}{4}$" × $26\frac{3}{8}$". Roland, Browse & Delbanco, London.

2 Birth, 1910. Oil, $25\frac{5}{8}$" × $35\frac{1}{8}$". Owned by the Artist.

3 Death (Candles in a Dark Street), 1908. Oil, $27\frac{1}{8}$" × $34\frac{1}{4}$". Owned by the artist.

4 My Studio, 1910. Oil, $23\frac{3}{4}$" × $28\frac{3}{4}$". Owned by the artist.

5 Portrait of My Sister, 1909. Oil, $36\frac{3}{8}$" × $18\frac{1}{8}$". Wallraf-Richartz-Museum (Haubrich Collection), Cologne.

6 The Wedding, 1910. Oil, $38\frac{5}{8}$" × 74". Owned by the artist.

7 Portrait of My Fiancée in Black Gloves, 1909. Oil, $34\frac{5}{8}$" × $25\frac{1}{4}$". Kunstmuseum, Basle.

8 Portrait of the Artist with Seven Fingers, 1911. Oil, $50\frac{3}{8}$" × $42\frac{1}{8}$". Municipal Museum (P. A. Regnault Collection), Amsterdam.

9 The Soldier drinks, 1912–13. Oil, $45\frac{7}{8}$" × $37\frac{1}{8}$". The Solomon R. Guggenheim Foundation, New York.

10 Study for *The Drunkard* (Interior), 1911–12. Gouache with Water-colour and Pencil, $9\frac{3}{8}$" × 12". Stuttgarter Kunstkabinett, Roman Norbert Ketterer, Stuttgart.

11 To Russia, Asses and Others, 1911. Oil, $61\frac{5}{8}$" × $48\frac{1}{8}$". Musée National d'Art Moderne, Paris.

12 Paris through the Window, 1913. Oil, 52" × $53\frac{7}{8}$". The Solomon R. Guggenheim Foundation, New York.

13 Calvary, 1912. Oil, $68\frac{1}{2}$" × $75\frac{1}{2}$". The Museum of Modern Art, New York.

14 Self-Portrait, 1914. Oil, $19\frac{3}{8}$" × $14\frac{3}{4}$". Collection Robert Buron, Paris.

15 The Birthday, 1915–23. Oil on cardboard, 31³/₄" × 39¹/₄".
Museum of Modern Art (Lillie P. Bliss Bequest), New York.

16 The Green Rabbi, 1914. Oil, 39¹/₄" × 31¹/₂". Charles Im Obersteg, Geneva.

17 Soldiers, 1914. Oil, 19⁵/₈" × 14³/₄". Private Collection, Paris.

18 Sketch for *The Revolution*, 1937. Oil, 19⁵/₈" × 39³/₄". Owned by the artist.

19 The Blue House, 1920. Oil, 26¹/₈" × 38¹/₄". Museum of Fine Arts, Liège.

20 Paysage cubiste, 1918. Oil, 39¹/₄" × 23¹/₈". Collection Mme Ida Meyer-Chagall, Berne.

21 Self-Portrait with a Wineglass, 1917. Oil, 92¹/₂" × 54".
Musée National d'Art Moderne, Paris.

22 The Violinist, 1912–13. Oil, 74" × 62¹/₂". Municipal Museum (P. A. Regnault Collection), Amsterdam.

23 Man with a Kid, 1919 (Sketch for a Play by Sholem Aleichem). 13³/₄" × 10".
Owned by the artist.

24 Lovers in a Garden, 1923. Oil, 31⁷/₈" × 25¹/₂". Municipal Museum (P. A. Regnault Collection), Amsterdam.

25 The Angel with Palette, 1926–36. Oil, 52" × 35³/₈". Owned by the artist.

26 Lovers on a Horse, 1931. Oil, 39³/₄" × 35". Municipal Museum (P. A. Regnault Collection), Amsterdam.

27 The Lovers in the Lilacs, 1931. Oil, 51" × 35".
Collection Richard Zeissler, New York.

28 The Lion who has grown old, from the Illustrations for La Fontaine's *Fables* (1927–31), Gouache.

29 The Ass and the little Dog, from the Illustrations for La Fontaine's *Fables* (1927–31), Gouache.

30 The Creation of Man, from the Illustrations for the *Bible*, 1930.
Gouache, 25" × 17³/₄".

31 Abraham entertaining the three Angels, from the Illustrations for the *Bible*, 1931.
Gouache.

32 The Violinist in the Snow, 1927, Gouache. Museum of Modern Art, New York.

33 Solitude, Study for the oil-painting, 1933. Private Collection, Tel Aviv.

34 The Bride's Chair, 1934. Oil, 39³/₈" × 37³/₈". Collection Baronne Lambert, Brussels.

35 The Three Candles, 1938–40. Oil, 50³/₄" × 37¹/₂".
Collection Mrs. Dewitt Wallace, Pleasantville, New York.

36 A ma femme, 1934–44. Oil, 51¹/₈" × 76¹/₂". Musée National d'Art Moderne, Paris.

37 Cello Player, 1939. Oil, 39¹/₂" × 28³/₄". Municipal Museum (P. A. Regnault Collection), Amsterdam.

38 White Crucifixion, 1938. Oil, 61" × 55". (Courtesy of The Art Institute of Chicago), Gift of Mrs. Alfred S. Alschuler.

39 Martyrdom, 1940. Oil, 64³/₄" × 44³/₄". Private Collection, France.

40 Between Darkness and Light (Dusk), 1938–43. Oil, 39¹/₄" × 28³/₄".
Collection Mme Ida Meyer-Chagall, Berne.

41 Time is a River without Banks, 1930–39. Oil, 40¹/₂" × 32⁵/₈".
Museum of Modern Art, New York.

42 Harlequin Family, 1942. Oil, Collection Pierre Matisse, New York.

43 In the Night, 1943. Oil, 18⁷/₈" × 20³/₈". Collection Louis E. Stern, New York.

44 War, 1943. Oil, 72³/₈" × 50³/₄". Musée National d'Art Moderne, Paris.

45 The Yellow Crucifixion, 1943. Oil, 56″ × 40″. Owned by the artist.
46 The Juggler, 1943. Oil, 43 1/2″ × 31″. The Art Institute of Chicago (Gift of Mrs. Gilbert W. Chapman).
47 Mexican Rooster, 1943. Gouache, 20 1/8″ × 29 1/8″. Collection Paul Hänggi, Basle.
48 Design for scenery for *Aleko* produced by the Ballet Theatre, Mexico City and New York, 1942. Gouache, 15 1/4″ × 22 1/2″. Museum of Modern Art, New York, Lillie P. Bliss Bequest, Theatre Art Collection.
49 Self-Portrait with Clock, 1947. Oil, 38 1/8″ × 28″. Owned by the artist.
50 Autour d'elle, 1945. Oil, 51 5/8″ × 42 7/8″. Musée National d'Art Moderne, Paris.
51 Nocturne, 1947. Oil, 35″ × 28 1/2″. Private Collection, France.
52 Curtain Design for *The Fire Bird*, 1945. Gouache, 14 3/4″ × 24 3/8″. Owned by the artist.
53 The Bare Cloud, 1945–46. Oil, 26″ × 34″. Private Collection, Paris.
54 The Siren, from the Illustrations for The Arabian Night's Entertainments, 1946–47. Gouache, Private Collection, Sweden.
55 The Blue Barque, 1951. Gouache, 15 3/8″ × 21 1/4″. Owned by the artist.
56 The Green Cock, 1949. Oil, 38 1/8″ × 29 7/8″. Collection Riccardo Gualino, Rome.
57 Landscape St. Jean Cap Ferrat, 1949. Gouache, 29 7/8″ × 22″. Collection Mme Ida Meyer-Chagall, Berne.
58 The Circus, 1950–52. Oil, 91″ × 68 1/2″. Owned by the artist.
59 The Black and Red World (Study for *The Red Sun*), 1949. Oil, 55″ × 38 5/8″. Municipal Museum, Amsterdam.
60 The Green Circus, 1950–55. Oil, 19 5/8″ × 23 5/8″. Galerie Maeght, Paris.
61 The Lovers, 1955–56. Oil, 59″ × 47 1/4″. Galerie Maeght, Paris.
62 Farmer, Fountain and Ass, Ceramic, Height 12 5/8″.
63 Cock, Nude and Lovers, Ceramic, Height 18 1/8″.
64 The Lovers, 1954–63. Oil, 21 5/8″ × 18″. Galerie Maeght, Paris.
65 Circus, 1964. Gouache, 19 7/8″ × 26 3/16″. Galerie Maeght, Paris.
66/67 Commedia dell'Arte, 1959. Oil, 99 1/4″ × 157 1/2″. State Theatre, Frankfurt a. M.
68/69 Chagall in front of the window (12′ × 15′) in the United Nations Building in New York dedicated to the memory of Dag Hammarskjöld, 1964.
70 Dome fresco in the Paris Opera, 1964.
71 Detail from the dome fresco in the Paris Opera.
72 Chagall at work on the ceiling paintings for the Paris Opera.

Sources of Illustrations

The in-text pictures on pages 33, 83, 87, 99, 118, 147 are reproduced, by kind permission, from the book *Marc Chagall, Das graphische Werk*, by Franz Meyer and Hans Bolliger, Hatje, Stuttgart 1957 (*Mark Chagall: The Graphic Work*, Thames & Hudson, London and Abrams, New York). We are indebted to the following publishers for permission to reproduce other illustrations.
R. Piper & Co., Munich: *Marc Chagall, Arabische Nächte*, Introduction by Kurt Moldovan (Ill. p. 126); Philosophical Library, New York: *Marc Chagall, His Life and Work*, by Isaac Kloomok (Ill. pp. 31, 37, 60); Editions des Trois Collines, Geneva-Paris: *Chagall ou l'orage enchanté*, by Raïssa Maritain (Ill. pp. 102, 108); Gustav Kiepenheuer, Potsdam: *Die Kunst Marc Chagalls*, by A. Efross and J. Tugendhold (Ill. pp. 22, 23, 29, 66).

Acknowledgment is also made to the Museum of Modern Art, New York, and the Art Institute of Chicago, Catalogue of the Chagall Exhibition 1946, by J. J. Sweeney (Ill. pp. 35, 58); the Stedelijk Museum, Amsterdam, and the Palais des Beaux-Arts, Brussels, Catalogue of the Chagall Exhibition 1957 (Ill. p. 71); the Albertina in Vienna, Catalogue of the Marc Chagall Exhibition 1953, Anton Schroll & Co., Vienna (Ill. p. 114); the Tate Gallery, London, Catalogue of the Chagall Exhibition 1948 (Ill. p. 125).

Photographs:

Archives photographiques, Paris: 4, 23, 25, 36, 44, 54, 56, 57. Berard & Fils, Nice: 52. Bildarchiv Rhein. Museum, Cologne: 5. Kurt Blum, Berne: IV, VI, VII, IX, X, XII, 62, 63, 64. Colin, Vence: 30, 58. Colten Photo, New York: 3, 42, 53. E. R. Dents, Philadelphia: 18. Joh. Enschedé en Zonen, Haarlem: II. Helga Fietz, Munich: VIII. R. Gauthier, Paris: 6, 43, 48. Louis Laniepce, Paris: V. Kunstmuseum Basle: 7. Galerie Pierre Matisse, New York: 11. Dr. te Neues & Co., Kempen: XI. Dr. Rathschlag, Cologne: I, III. REP, Boulogne-sur-Seine: 29. Roland, Browse & Delbanco, London: 1. M. Routhier, Paris: 47, 55, 59. Stedelijk Museum, Amsterdam: 24, 26, 37. Soichi Sunami, New York: 15, 41. Marc Vaux, Paris: 16, 27, 31, 32, 33.

The plates

1 Family, 1908

2 Birth, 1910

3 Death, 1908

4 My Studio, 1910

5 Portrait of My Sister, 1909

6 The Wedding, 1910

7 Portrait of My Fiancée in Black Gloves, 1909

8 Portrait of the Artist with Seven Fingers, 1911

9 The Soldier drinks, 1912–13

10 Study for *The Drunkard*, 1911–12

11 To Russia, Asses and Others, 1911

12 Paris through the Window, 1913

13 Calvary, 1912

14 Self-Portrait, 1914

15 The Birthday, 1915–23

16 The Green Rabbi, 1914

17 Soldiers, 1914

18 Sketch for *The Revolution,* 1937

19 The Blue House, 1920

20 Paysage cubiste, 1918

21 Self-Portrait with a Wineglass, 1917

22 The Violinist, 1912–13

23 Man with a Kid, 1919. Sketch for a Play by Sholem Aleichem

24 Lovers in a Garden, 1923

25 The Angel with Palette, 1927–36

26 Lovers on a Horse, 1931

27 The Lovers in the Lilacs, 1931

28 The *Fables* of La Fontaine, 1927–31. The Lion who has grown old

29 The *Fables* of La Fontaine, 1927–31. The Ass and the little Dog

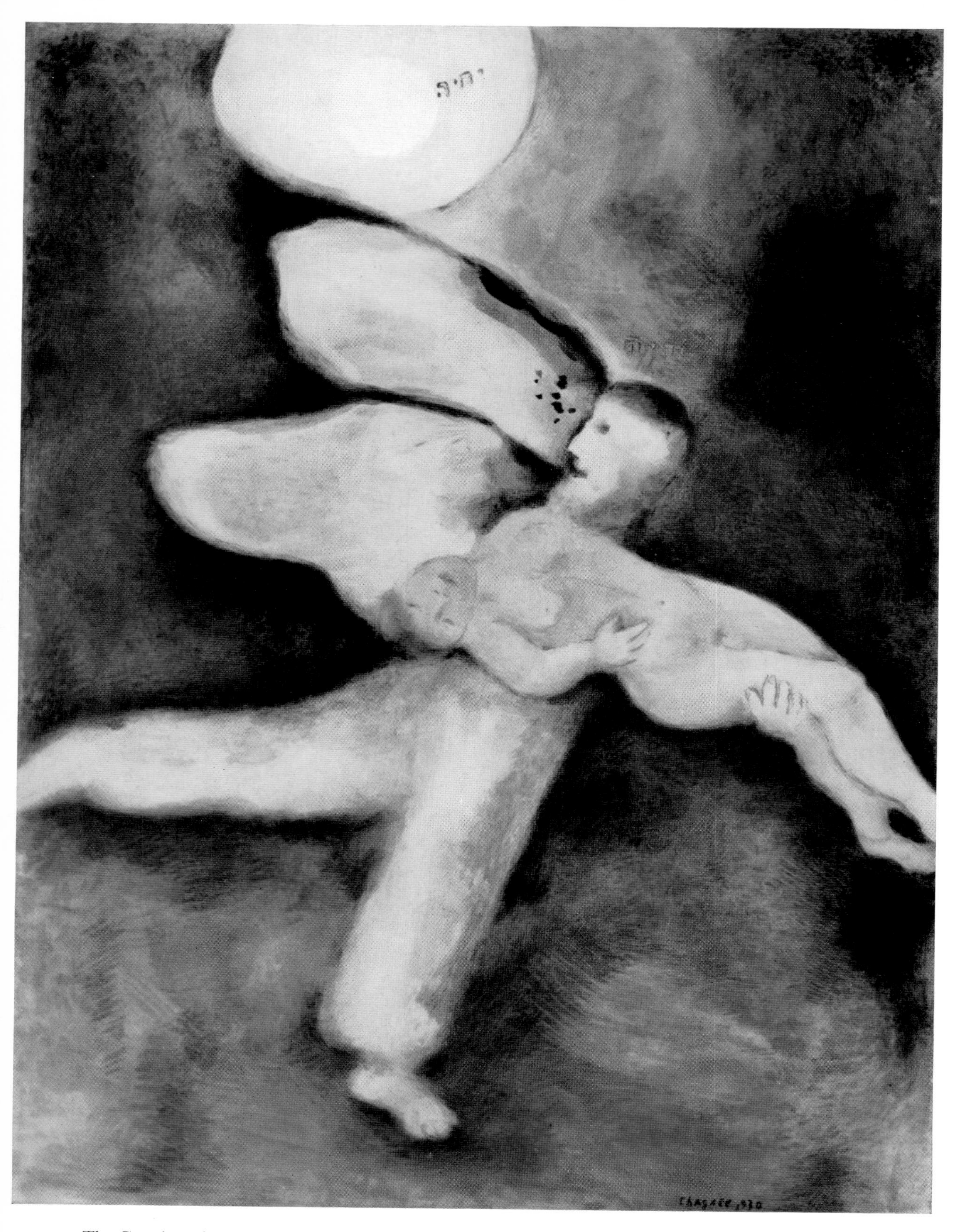

30 The Creation of Man, 1930. Illustrations for the *Bible*

31 Abraham entertaining the three Angels, 1931. Illustrations for the *Bible*

32 The Violinist in the Snow, 1927

33 Solitude, 1933

34 The Bride's Chair, 1934

35 The Three Candles, 1938-40

36 A ma femme, 1933–44

37 Cello Player, 1939

chagall
MARC 1939

38 White Crucifixion. 1938

39 Martyrdom, 1940

40 Between Darkness and Light, 1938–43

41 Time is a River without Banks, 1930–39

42 Harlequin Family, 1942

43 In the Night, 1943

44 War, 1943

45 The Yellow Crucifixion, 1943

46 Thn Juggler, 1943

47 Mexican Rooster, 1943

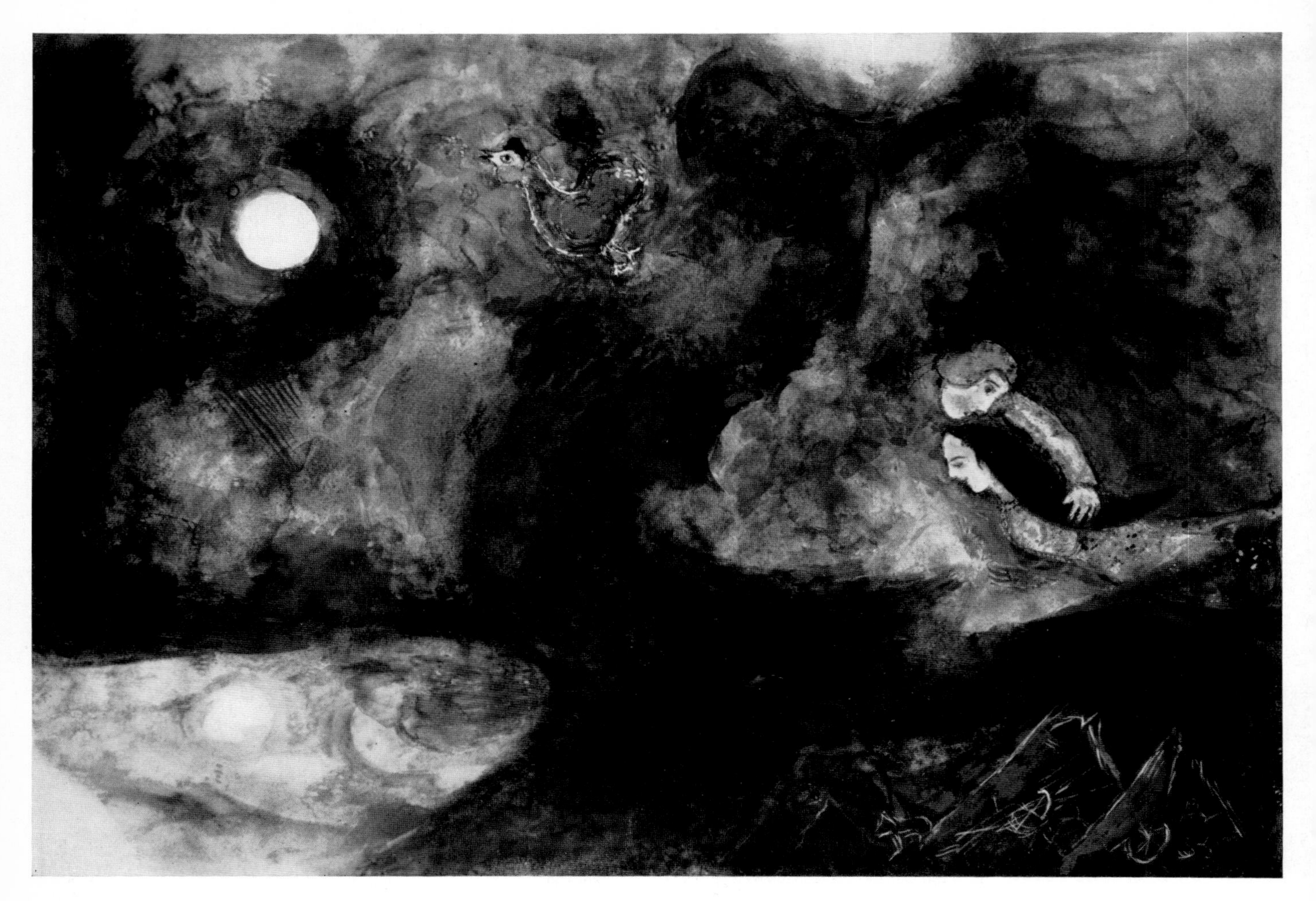

48 Design for scenary for *Aleko*, 1942

49 Self-Portrait with Clock, 1947

50 Autour d'elle, 1945

51 Nocturne, 1947

52 Curtain for *The Fire Bird*, 1945

53 The Bare Cloud, 1945–46

54 The Siren, 1946–47. Arabian Nights' Entertainments

55 The Blue Barque, 1951

56 The Green Cock, 1949

57 St. Jean Cap Ferrat, 1949

Chagall

59 The Black and Red World, 1949. Study for *The Red Sun*

58 The Circus, 1950–52

60 The Green Circus, 1950–55

61 The Lovers, 1955–56

Marc
Chagall

62 Farmer, Fountain and Ass

63 Cock, Nude and Lovers

64 The Lovers, 1954–63

65 Circus, 1964

66-67 *Commedia dell'Arte*, 1959

68-69 Chagall in front of the window in the United Nations Building in New York dedicated to the memory of Dag Hammerskjöld, 1964

70 Dome fresco in the Paris Opéra, 1964

71 Details from the dome fresco in the Paris Opéra

72 Chagall at work on the ceiling paintings for the Paris Opéra